Let's Read Latin

Let's Read Latin
Introduction to the Language of the Church

Ralph McInerny

Second Edition
expanded and revised

Dumb Ox Books
South Bend, Indiana
1995

6 7 8 9 10 11 12   10 09 08 07 06 05 04

For Mother Angelica
Mulier fortis

Contents

Preface to the Second Edition

THIS LITTLE BOOK has been well received during the first five years of its existence, and it goes forth now in a second expanded and corrected edition. That so many have found it useful is gratifying. The approach taken here remains unique among the Latin books available. The intended reader is one who wants to get the hang of Church Latin. This book plunges him immediately into the texts he wants to learn to read. Grammar and syntax are provided on the margins of that focus. This completely reverses the usual practice, where grammars concentrate on grammar fairly abstractly and, when readings are given, they merely illustrate the grammar.

The *Vademecum* that makes up Chapter 22 appeared in late printings of the first edition. A number of knowledgeable readers have drawn my attention to errors and misprints, and I am most grateful for their help. As Horace said, *etiam Homerus dormitat*, and I'm no Homer. Maybe a pop fly. In any case, I think the book is now free of error but, should anyone come across an infelicity, I urge him to let me know. It is a risky thing to be author and editor and co-publisher all at once (My partner in Dumb Ox Books is Bruce Fingerhut. He is the ox.) The authorial eye is notoriously blind to misprints and mistakes in a text, seeing what is meant to be there rather than what is.

Needless to say this is the most rudimentary of introductions. I would not call it Latin for Dummies, if only to stay out of legal trouble, but it has the same modestly liminal aim of that series of self-help books. Some come to this book as accomplished Latinists. Others are ecclesiastically monolingual. My hope is that every reader will find this book useful in familiarizing himself with the language that the Church has used from the beginning, continues to use and, *deo volente*, will use until the end of time. I won't be around to verify that, but maybe you will. Let me know, in Latin, which is the language spoken where I hope to be.

Ralph McInerny
January 2000

Original Preface

AMONG THE UNINTENDED EFFECTS of Vatican II has been the almost complete disappearance of Latin. Once we spoke of the Church of the Latin Rite. Now it is as if there is something wrong with Latin. Quite apart from the practical wisdom of the absence of Latin from today's liturgy, it is clear that without a knowledge of Latin, much of the Catholic patrimony will be closed off to the present generation.

It is of course silly to suggest that the Mass said in English or other vernacular languages is somehow less the Mass. One can champion Latin for the wrong reasons. Love of Latin can and ought to be something a good deal more than an expression of nostalgia or of bad theology. For centuries the thought and worship of the Church was conducted in Latin. The language of Vatican II was Latin, and it was in this language that its sixteen documents were issued. Those of us in whose hearts the cadences of Latin were engraved many years ago can summon them still. But there are many who want to acquire at least some beginning of an understanding and appreciation of Latin as the language of the Church. This little book responds to that desire.

Given the presumed aim of the reader, this book seeks to plunge immediately into prayers and scriptural and liturgical passages. The grammar and syntax of Latin are learned as the *sine qua non* of grasping the meaning of a prayer or psalm or hymn. When I began the study of Latin, in September 1942 at Nazareth Hall, we devoted a full year to an abstract study of grammar and syntax. By the time we turned, as sophomores, to the text of Caesar, our first zeal had been sorely tried. This book will sugar-coat the abstract with the contemporary benefit of mastering an essential element in our Catholic patrimony. We shall move, as toward our goal, to the reading of a passage from the *Summa theologiae* of Saint Thomas Aquinas.

Lesson One

Pater Noster

THIS IS HOW JESUS, IN MATTHEW 6:9–13, taught his disciples to pray:

1. **Pater noster**
2. **qui es in coelis**
3. **sanctificetur nomen tuum**
4. **adveniat regnum tuum**
5. **fiat voluntas tua**
6. **sicut in coelo et in terra.**
7. **Panem nostrum quotidianum da nobis hodie**
8. **et dimitte nobis debita nostra**
9. **sicut et nos dimittimus debitoribus nostris**
10. **et ne nos inducas in tentationem**
11. **sed libera nos a malo.**

That is how it sounds in Latin. Of course you are familiar with it in its English version:

[1] Our Father
[2] who art in heaven
[3] hallowed be thy name
[4] thy kingdom come
[5] thy will be done
[6] on earth as it is in heaven.
[7] Give us this day our daily bread
[8] and forgive us our trespasses
[9] as we forgive those who trespass against us
[10] and lead us not into temptation
[11] but deliver us from evil.

If we put these versions together, the English will help us understand the prayer in its Latin version. The prayer has been divided into numbered lines for purposes of easy comparison.

1. **Pater noster**
[1] Our Father

2. **qui es in coelis**
[2] who art in heaven

3. **sanctificetur nomen tuum**
[3] hallowed by thy name

4. **adveniat regnum tuum**
[4] thy kingdom come

5. **fiat voluntas tua**
[5] thy will be done

6. **sicut in coelo et in terra**
[6] on earth as it is in heaven.

If we were to put the English words in the order of their Latin equivalents, something familiar would become strange.

1. **Pater noster**
   Father our

2. **qui es in coelis**
   who art in heaven

3. **sanctificetur nomen tuum**
   blessed be name yours

4. **adveniat regnum tuum**
   let come reign yours

5. **fiat voluntas tua**
   let be done will yours

6. **sicut in coelo et in terra**
   as in heaven and on earth.

This rearrangement enables us to see word for word correlations:

father = **pater**
our = **noster**
who = **qui**
art = **es**
in = **in**
heaven = **coelis**
hallowed be = **sanctificetur**
name = **nomen**
your = **tuum**

Father is a noun, a name; a noun signifies something or someone. Nouns are used in various ways.

Sometimes we use nouns to say something *about* what is named. The father has a daughter: **Pater filiam habet.**

Sometimes what is named is taken to have or *possess* something in the sense of "the father's daughter." In English, this is indicated by apostrophe + s ['s] after the noun. Latin does it differently: **filia patris.**

Just as the difference in English is signaled by what happens at the end of the word, so too in Latin. Indeed, word ending as indicating different uses of a noun are far more frequent in Latin— so frequent in fact that we can say they characterize it. Latin is an INFLECTED language.

In a prayer, we are speaking directly to God, addressing him. No difference shows up at the end of a noun in its talking-about use (**Pater noster est in coelis:** *Our father is in heaven*) and in its talking-to use (**Pater noster qui es in coelis:** *Our Father who art in heaven*). Look for the clues to the talking-about (NOMINATIVE) and talking-to (VOCATIVE) use. If the difference is not found at the end of the word, we will notice differences in the sentences in which they occur (**est** and **es**, for example, and the need for **qui** in the vocative).

If **pater** is a noun, **es** is a verb, a form of the verb to be [= **esse**], the most common verb in any language. How does **es** differ from **est**?

In English we say: I am, you are, he is; we are, you are, they are. In Latin we say: **sum, es, est, sumus, estis, sunt.**

Lots of changes in both languages. Often in English a verb does not change as used of one or more persons:

I come, you come, he comes, we come, you come, they come.

Only when we say that he, she, or it is on the way do we alter *come* to *comes*. This is what we know when we know English; we don't ask why. Without the addition of I, you, he, and so forth, the meaning would not come through to us. Latin usually omits pronouns—I, you, he, she, we, they. By altering the end of the verb, it tells us which pronoun is implied.

Venio, venis, venit, venimus, venitis, veniunt.

Thus, in Latin, we watch the way words end, both nouns and verbs, to understand what is being said. The occurrence of **es** rather than **est** in the prayer Jesus taught us alerts us to the fact that we are addressing God. It is not **Pater est** but **Pater es. Qui es in coelis.**

Adjectives

You might underline in the Latin version of the prayer recurrent words, counting as the same words instances where the same stem has different endings. What do you find?

noster, nostrum, nostra, nostris
coelis, coelo
tuum, tua
nobis, nos

The variations **noster, nostrum, nostra, nostros** are due to the nouns this possessive adjective (our) is attached to [that is what adjective means, as we will learn: **ad-jacere**].

Nouns in Latin are either masculine, feminine, or neuter, and usually their endings tell us what their gender is. Their adjectives will tell us this almost always. Further, since nouns are inflected, that is, have end-changes to tell us how they are being used, their adjectives must follow suit so we will know what they are attached to.

Pater noster
panem nostrum
debita nostra
debitoribus nostris

Pater noster: pater is masculine and is being used in the prayer in the talking-to way; **noster** here is also masculine and vocative.

Panem nostrum is different. *Give us bread.* Bread is the object of the verb. Something is being done to what is named; it is the object of giving. This case of the noun is called the ACCUSATIVE or OBJECTIVE case. **Nostrum** is the masculine objective or accusative case of the adjective **noster.**

So too in **debita nostra,** our trespasses are being talked about: **debitum** is the neuter noun meaning debt, something owed. **Debitum nostrum** would be the nominative case, singular: our debt. **Debita nostra** is the plural of this neuter noun: our debts.

In **debitoribus nostris,** we have one word related to **debitum** and another to **noster.** First of all, it must be said that both are plural—*our debtors*— and both are in the DATIVE case. *As we forgive our debtors.*

Coelis, coelo. The nominative case of this neuter noun is **coelum,** *heaven.* In the prayer, we are addressing our Father in heaven. The preposition in here governs the case, indicating, among other things, where the subject being talked about is. The term is used first in the ablative plural, **coelis,** and then in the ablative singular, **coelo,** but of course each time is introduced by the preposition **in,** which alerts us, along with the ending, as to how the noun is being used.

Tuum, tua. Noster is a possessive adjective, so too is **tuum.** As an adjective, it will agree with the noun with which it is joined in gender, number, and case. *That is the rule for adjectives.* It is because **nomen** is a singular neuter noun, which is here used in its talking-to or vocative case, that we want its adjective to be vocative, neuter, and singular. **Tuus, tua, tuum** are the masculine, feminine, and neuter nominative singular forms of the adjective meaning *your;* so the prayer uses **tuum,** the vocative and nominative forms being, as we noted, the same.

Nobis, nos. The first form of the word is dative: *give to us our daily bread.* The second is the objective case: *forgive us.*

Paradigms displaying the declension of these possessive adjectives are found in the appendix. Why DECLENSION? The word suggests a decline, a falling away. The talking-about or nominative form of the noun is taken to be the standard or default instance; the other forms or cases—fallings—are seen as cascading away from the nominative. Keeping an eye out for the metaphors grammar uses provides special delights. (The answer to the question, "What does 'paradigms' stand for?" is not twenty cents.)

By picking out similar forms of words occurring in the **Pater**

noster, we have learned essential features of Latin. Its nouns and adjectives are declined; paradigms arrange different forms of nouns and adjectives insofar as uses secondary to the nominative are seen as falling away, or declining, from it.

Nouns are masculine, feminine, or neuter.

The cases of nouns are usually indicated by a specific ending of the common root: **pa-ter; pa-tris; pa-tri; pa-trem.**

Adjectives agree with the nouns they modify in gender, number and case.

Verbs

Let's look now at the verbs in the **Pater noster.** First, we will make a list of the verbs in the prayer, omitting the forms of the verb to be = **esse.**

sanctificetur
adveniat
fiat
da
dimitte
dimittimus
inducas
libera

Let us begin with what are clearly two forms of the same verb, **dimitte** and **dimittimus.** In the prayer, when we ask God to take away our sins, we use an imperative or commanding form of the verb. We are asking God to *do* something: to forgive. **Da,** *give,* is the same form of a different verb, the imperative of **dare.**

Notice that when we speak about a verb, we use one of its forms by preference: thus I have spoken of the verb to be, **esse;** and in speaking of the verb to give, in Latin as in English I use the infinitive form, **dare.** The infinitive form of the verb we have decided to begin with is **dimittere,** *to forgive.*

Just as nouns are inflected, so verbs are altered so that we can tell how they are being used. What we have to know in order to understand a particular use of a verb is the person, number, and tense.

Earlier, we gave the Latin equivalent of:

I come, you come, he comes, we come, you come, they come.

	Singular	*Plural*
1.	**venio**	**venimus**
2.	**venis**	**venitis**
3.	**venit**	**veniunt**

If we did this for **dimittere** we would have:

	Singular	*Plural*
1.	**dimitto**	**dimittimus**
2.	**dimittis**	**dimittitis**
3.	**dimittit**	**dimittunt**

Of the forms of **dimittere** that show up in the prayer, the commanding or imperative form, **dimitte,** is addressed to God; in this context it would be better to call it the DEPRECATIVE form. We are asking, not telling, God to do something. On the other hand, **dimittimus** refers to our forgiving: it means *we forgive*, as the paradigm above would indicate.

Da, we have already noted, is the commanding, or deprecative, form of **dare,** *to give.*

I give, you give, he gives, we give, you give, they give

	Singular	*Plural*
1.	**do**	**damus**
2.	**das**	**datis**
3.	**dat**	**dant**

Libera is the same form as **da** and **dimitte,** namely, the imperative. We are asking God to free us or deliver us from evil.

I free, you free, he frees, we free, you free, they free

	Singular	*Plural*
1.	**libero**	**liberamus**
2.	**liberas**	**liberatis**
3.	**liberat**	**liberant**

You will wonder why dimitte has a different ending than **da** and **libera.** Latin verbs are gathered into groups or CONJUGATIONS, of which there are four kinds—not counting the other kinds. That is, what are called regular verbs are of four kinds, but there are irregular verbs as well.

For now, all we need notice is that there are three kinds of regular verbs in the **Pater noster.**

Perhaps in doing crossword puzzles you have encountered a clue for a four-letter word described as familiar from beginning latin. The word is **amat.** The verb *to love,* **amare,** is taken to stand for all regular verbs of a certain kind.

Singular	*Plural*
1. **amo,** *I love*	**amamus,** *we love*
2. **amas,** *you love*	**amatis,** *you love*
3. **amat,** *he loves*	**amant,** *they love*

Like **amare** are **sanctificare, dare,** and **liberare.** A clue to their kind—called the First Conjugation or A Conjugation —is the presence of a in their stem. On this pattern, you can locate **inducas,** *you lead into.* And we already have seen that **libera** and **da** are imperative forms of A or First Conjugation verbs.

What in the world is **sanctificetur?** Two things are important to notice about it. It is a verb that expresses something to be done to or for the one referred to by the noun governing the verb; and it does not signify something being done so much as it expresses the hope that something will or may be done.

When a verb expresses an actual state of affairs, or describes some activity of the subject, it is said to indicate something; this manner or mode is called the INDICATIVE mood of the verb. The other mood is called the SUBJUNCTIVE, which can be exemplified in English by "Would it were so!" or "May all your troubles be little ones."

Sanctificetur expresses such a mood of the verb.

But it also expresses an activity to be done to the subject that governs it. Who is that subject? Our Father. Or, more precisely, His name. We are asking that His name be hallowed, recognized as holy. His name is not doing something here (i.e., it is not ACTIVE, but rather is PASSIVE), but we express subjunctively that something might be done to it: that His Name be hallowed.

Sanctificetur is then a subjunctive and passive form of the A or First Conjugation verb **sanctificare.**

Adveniat, *may it come*; *thy kingdom come* can be expanded into *may thy kingdom come.* This is a subjunctive form of the verb *to come* or *to arrive,* **advenire,** the verb from which we get *Advent.* This is an I or Fourth Conjugation verb, as a glance at its stem indicates. It is a compound verb, made up of **ad,** *to or toward,* and **venire,** *come.* Notice the use of **venire** in speaking of the impaneling of a jury. We have already conjugated **venire** above, so we know that the present tense of **advenire** will be:

Singular	Plural
1. advenio	advenimus
2. advenis	advenitis
3. advenit	adveniunt

Adveniat is the third person singular present tense subjunctive form of the verb. *May it,* that is, *thy kingdom, come.*

Fiat is the third person singular subjunctive of an irregular verb, not the brand of an Italian automobile. Actually it is both. In Genesis, when God says "Let there be light," the Latin reads **fiat lux.** You will be able to think of English uses of this Latin word, as when we say that something came about by someone's fiat.

Nouns

We have already said many things about nouns. They are the subject of verbs, and adjectives must agree with the nouns they modify in gender, number, and case. The rule is intelligible insofar as we know what the gender and number and case of nouns are. And we do. We know that nouns in Latin are masculine, feminine, or neuter. We know that they are singular or plural. We know that their endings alert us to whether the thing named by the noun is doing something or is the object of a doing or is the possessor of something or is that by which or where some action comes about.

What we know can be summarized by taking a noun from the **Pater noster.** Let's take **voluntas,** *will.* It occurs in the prayer in the nominative singular.

Third Declension

	Singular	Plural
Nominative	voluntas	voluntates
Genitive	voluntatis	voluntatum
Dative	voluntati	voluntatibus
Accusative	voluntatem	voluntates
Ablative	voluntate	voluntatibus

There are four kinds or conjugations of regular verbs, and there are five declensions of nouns. **Voluntas** belongs to the Third Declension. Let us have before us an example of a noun in the First Declension. An example is **ecclesia,** *church.*

First Declension

	Singular	*Plural*
Nominative	ecclesia	ecclesiae
Genitive	ecclesiae	ecclesiarum
Dative	ecclesiae	ecclesiis
Accusative	ecclesiam	ecclesias
Ablative	ecclesia	ecclesiis

The **Pater Noster** has given us a first entry into the language of the Church. We now know all sorts of things about Latin. That is not the point of the prayer, of course, but we can continue to use it as we are meant to—as a prayer.

Vocabulary

There are forty-nine words in the **Pater Noster,** but some of them occur more than once or are variations on a noun or verb stem. You have learned the following thirty words.

a, prep., *away, from*
advenire, vb. (4), *to come, arrive*
coelum, coeli, n., *heaven*
dare, vb. (1),[1] *to give*
debitor, debitoris, n. (3), masc., *debtors*
debitum, debiti, n., neut. (2), *debt*
dimittere, vb. (3), *forgive, dismiss*
esse, irreg. vb., *to be*
et, conj., *and*
fieri, irreg. vb., *become*
hodie, adv., *today*
in, prep., *in*
inducere, vb. (3), *lead into*
liberare, vb. (1), *to free, deliver*

---

1   The number in parentheses refers to the conjugation of the verb or the declension of the noun.

malum, mali, n. (2), masc., *evil*
nomen, nominis, n. (3), neut., *name*
nos, nobis, pers. pron., *we, us*
noster, nostra, nostrum, adj., *our*
panis, panis, n. (3), masc., *bread*
Pater, patris, n. (3), masc., *father*
qui, quae, quod, rel. pron., *who, which*
quotidianus, -a, -um, adj., *daily*
regnum, regni, n. (2), neut., *reign, kingdom*
sanctificare, vb. (1), *to hallow, bless, make holy*
sed, conj., *but*
sicut, adv., *just as*
tentatio, tentationis, n. (3), fem., *temptation, trial*
terra, terrae, n. (1), fem., *earth*
tuus, tua, tuum, adj., *your*
voluntas, voluntatis, n. (3), fem., *will*

Lesson Two

Ave Maria

NOW THAT WE KNOW THE PATER NOSTER, we need only learn the Ave Maria, and we will be able to say the Rosary in Latin. Just as the Lord's Prayer is given us in Scripture, so too, in large part, is the Angelic Salutation or Hail Mary. The first half of the prayer is made up of the angel's declaration to Mary and Elizabeth's greeting to her cousin.

1. **Ave Maria**
2. **gratia plena**
3. **Dominus tecum**
4. **benedicta tu in mulieribus**
5. **et benedictus fructus ventris tui, Jesus.**
6. **Sancta Maria,**
7. **mater Dei**
8. **ora pro nobis peccatoribus**
9. **nunc et in hora mortis nostrae.**

[1] Hail Mary
[2] full of grace
[3] the Lord is with thee
[4] blessed art thou amongst women
[5] and blessed is the fruit of thy womb, Jesus.
[6] Holy Mary
[7] mother of God
[8] pray for us sinners
[9] now and at the hour of our death.

As with the Lord's Prayer, if we should make the English match the Latin words, the order would be odd.

1. **Ave Maria**
[1] Hail Mary

2. **gratia plena**
[2] grace full

3. **dominus tecum**
[3] Lord you-with

4. **benedicta tu in mulieribus**
[4] blessed you among women

5. **et benedictus fructus ventris tui, Jesus.**
[5] and blessed the fruit of womb yours, Jesus.

6. **Sancta Maria**
[6] Holy Mary

7. **mater Dei**
[7] mother of God

8. **ora pro nobis peccatoribus**
[8] pray for us sinners

9. **nunc et in hora mortis nostrae.**
[9] now and in the hour of death our.

Just as the angel and Elizabeth addressed Mary, so this whole prayer is addressed to her. Thus, we will expect nouns referring to Mary to be in the talking-to, or vocative, case rather than the talking-of, or nominative, case. However, as we have already seen, there is no change of ending to signal this. But of course we are alerted by the opening word, **ave,** hail, that the person Mary is being spoken to, interceded. Both **Maria,** and **Mater** are in the vocative case.

Gratia plena. This is somewhat unusual. **Plena** is the singular feminine form of the adjective, **plenus, plena, plenum.** It has the gender and number and case that it does because it modifies **Maria.** Now, although the English has "full of grace," the Latin is not **gratiae plena,** but **gratia plena.** Grammarians call this the ABLATIVE OF DESCRIPTION. This means that **gratia** and **plena,** despite appearances, are not in the same case. **Plena** is not an adjective modifying **gratia** such that the phrase would mean "full grace"; rather it modifies **Maria,** meaning it is in the vocative case; **gratia** is in the ablative case.

First Declension Adjective

Nominative	gratia
Genitive	gratiae
Dative	gratiae
Accusative	gratiam
Ablative	gratia

The meaning of the phrase therefore is "full as to grace."

Dominus tecum. Perhaps you expected **Dominus cum te.** Well, just as Spanish and other modern languages do, Latin sometimes places the preposition after the noun it goes with rather than before. **Dominus vobiscum,** *The Lord be with you,* is another instance of this.

Benedicta tu in mulieribus. The adjective agrees in gender, number, and case with the noun it modifies, namely, **Maria; tu** is the personal pronoun, second person singular, since we are addressing Mary. The preposition **in** governs the ablative case, in the plural, to express Mary's preeminence among all women.

Third Declension

	Singular	*Plural*
Nominative	mulier	mulieres
Genitive	mulieris	mulierum
Dative	mulieri	mulieribus
Accusative	mulierem	mulieres
Ablative	muliere	mulieribus

Benedictus fructus ventris tui, Jesus. The subject of this clause is the noun **fructus,** which is masculine and occurs here in the nominative case, singular. Accordingly, its adjective must also be nominative singular masculine, and so it is, **benedictus.** We have just encountered this same adjective in its feminine singular vocative form modifying **Maria** in line 4. The term for womb is, oddly enough, masculine, **venter, ventris, ventri, ventrem, ventre** in the singular, and we have it here in the genitive case, indicating that something is of it, or possessed by it. Mary's child, Jesus, is here metaphorically spoken of as the fruit, **fructus,** of her womb.

That is the first part of the prayer, an amalgam, as we noted, of two Scriptural passages, Luke 1:28 and Luke 1:42. The second half of the prayer is of non-Scriptural origin, that is, is not quoting Scripture.

Sancta Maria. We continue to address Mary, so both the noun and the adjective are feminine singular vocative.

Mater Dei. The term **Mater** agrees with **Maria,** but it is a noun, not an adjective. Grammarians will say that it is in apposition to the first noun, which is a technical way of saying that one noun is placed next to another. They are linked by the fact that both refer (and in the talking-to mode, vocatively) to the same person, Mary. **Dei** is the genitive case of **Deus,** a masculine noun.

Ora pro nobis. Ora is the imperative or deprecative of the first conjugation verb **orare,** the present tense of which is this:

Present Tense 1st Conjugation

Singular	*Plural*
1. **oro,** *I pray*	**oramus,** *we pray*
2. **oras,** *you pray*	**oratis,** *you pray*
3. **orat,** *she prays*	**orant,** *they pray*

pro is a preposition meaning for or on behalf of, and it governs the ablative case. Here it governs the plural ablative of **peccator.**

Third Declension

	Singular	*Plural*
Nominative	peccator	peccatores
Genitive	peccatoris	peccatorum
Dative	peccatori	peccatoribus
Accusative	peccatorem	peccatores
Ablative	peccatore	peccatoribus

Nunc et in hora mortis nostrae. The adverb **nunc,** now, modifies the imperative, **ora,** pray; we ask Mary to pray for us sinners now and then add, **et in hora mortis nostrae,** and in the hour of our death. The preposition **in** governs the ablative case of the feminine noun **hora,** and the rest is in the genitive because the hour in question is that of our death. **Mortis,** accordingly, is in the genitive or possessive case, and so is its adjective, **nostrae,** the singular genitive feminine of **noster, nostra, nostrum,** our friends from the **Pater Noster.**

Vocabulary

There are 30 words in the **Ave Maria,** the following of which are new to us.

Ave, imperative of **aveo,** *hail*
benedictus, benedicta, benedictum, adj., *blessed*
cum, prep., *with*
Deus, dei, n. (2), masc., *God*
Dominus, domini, n. (2), masc., *lord*
fructus, fructus, n. (4), masc., *fruit*
gratia, gratiae, n. (1), fem., *grace*
hora, horae, n. (1), fem., *hour*
mater, matris, n. (2), fem., *mother*
mors, mortis, n. (3), fem., *death*
nobis, ablative of **nos,** we, *us*
nunc, adv., *now*
orare, A-vb. (1), *to pray*
peccator, peccatoris, n. (3) masc., *sinner*
plenus, plena, plenum, adj., *full*
pro, prep., *for, on behalf of*
sanctus, sancta, sanctum, adj., *holy*
tu, pron., *thou, you*
tuus, tua, tuum, adj., *your* (singular of **vester, vestra, vestrum**).
venter, ventris, n. (3), masc., *womb*

The Angelus

V. **Angelus Domini nuntiavit[1] Mariae;**
R. **Et concepit[2] de Spiritu Sancto.**
   Ave Maria.
V. **Ecce ancilla Domini;**
R. **Fiat mihi secundum verbum tuum.[3] Ave Maria.**

---

1   Third person singular of the perfect active of the 1st conjugation verb
     nuntiare. Ancilla, -ae, f. (1), *handmaid.* **Mariae,** dative singular.
2   From **concipere** (3); the subject of **concepit** is Maria, understood. .
3   **Fiat** is the present subjunctive of **fio, fieri, factus sum,** the passive of
     facere (3). *Let it happen, let it be done;* **mihi** is dative, *to me;* **secundum**
     here means *according to,* following, **verbum, -i** (2), neuter, *word.*

V. Et verbum caro[4] factum est;

R. Et habitavit[5] in nobis.

Ave Maria.

V. Ora pro nobis, sancta Dei genetrix;

R. Ut digni efficiamur[6] promissionibus Christi.

Oremus.

Gratiam tuam, quaesumus Domine, mentibus nostris in-
funde:[7] ut qui, Angelo nuntiante,[8] Christum Filli tui incar-
nationem cognovimus, per passionem eius et crucem ad
resurrectionis gloriam perducamur.[9] Per eumdem Christum Dominum nostrum. Amen.

---

4   **Caro, carnis,** is the predicate noun and **verbum** is the subject of the
     past passive **factum est;** the participle agreeing in gender with the
     noun.

5   Third person singular, perfect active of **habitare** (1): *to dwell or live
     in.*

6   First person plural present subjunctive passive of **efficere:** *that we
     may be made* **digni,** *worthy,* followed by the ablative plural of **promis-
     sio, -ionis,** f.

7   Imperative or deprecative of **infundere:** *to pour forth.* The object of
     the verb is **gratiam. Mentibus** is the dative plural, modified by
     nostris: *into our minds.*

8   **Angelo nuntiante**—ablative absolute of the noun and the present
     participle: *the angel announcing,* or: *it being announced by an angel.*

9   Another passive subjunctive in the first person plural, of **perducere**
     (3); **Christum** is the object of **cognovimus,** *we came to know,* perfect
     of **cognoscere** (3).

The Magnificat

MARY RESPONDS TO HER COUSIN Elizabeth's greeting with a canticle which has become part of the liturgy. It became a fixture of the canonical hour of Vespers. The text is found in Luke 1:46–55.

1. Magnificat anima mea Dominum
2. et exsultavit spiritus meus in Deo salvatore meo,
3. quia respexit humilitatem ancillae suae.
4. Ecce enim ex hoc beatam me dicent omnes generationes,
5. quia fecit mihi magna, qui potens est,
6. et sanctum nomen eius,
7. et misericordia eius in progenies et progenies
8. timentibus eum.
9. Fecit potentiam in brachio suo,
10. dispersit superbos mente cordis sui;
11. deposuit potentes de sede
12. et exaltavit humiles;
13. esurientes implevit bonis
14. et divites dimisit inanes.
15. Suscepit Israel puerum suum,
16. recordatus misericordiae,
17. sicut locutus est ad patres nostros,
18. Abraham et semini eius in saecula.

Here is the **Magnificat** in English:

[1] My soul magnifies the Lord
[2] and my spirit rejoices in God my savior,
[3] who had regard for his handmaid's humility.
[4] For behold henceforth all generations will call me blessed,
[5] because he who is powerful has done great things for me,
[6] and holy is his name,
[7] and his mercy is from generation to generation
[8] for those who fear him.

[9] He made powerful his arm
[10] and dismissed the proud in the conceit of their heart;
[11] unseating the powerful
[12] and raising up the humble;
[13] he filled the hungry with good things
[14] and sent the rich away empty.
[15] He has helped Israel his son
[16] mindful of his mercy,
[17] as he spoke to our fathers,
[18] to Abraham and his seed forever.

A Song of Grateful Praise

Mary's heart is full of gratitude. Her soul gives thanks to the Lord, her spirit exults in God who is her savior because he has taken notice of her lowliness. Because of the great things God has done for her, all future generations will call her blessed. And we think of the Ave Maria, a prayer which, at every moment during the last two milennia, has been on someone's lips.

Mary then enumerates the basis for her gratitude and, in doing so, lays out the paradox of the New Covenant. God has put down the proud, unseated the powerful and raised up the humble; he has fed the hungry and sent the rich away empty-handed. The fulfillment of the prophecy made to Abraham and to other fathers is at hand,.

Past Tense

All the verbs in the Pater Noster and in the **Ave Maria** are in the present tense. In the **Magnificat**, we encounter a whole string of verbs used in the past tense: **exsultavit, respexit, fecit, dispersit, deposuit, exsaltavit, implevit, dimisit, locutus est.** It will be the chief burden of this lesson to gain some clarity about how Latin expresses past events.

There are three tenses of time—the past, the present, and the future. The linguistic expression of time is somewhat more complex. Latin has several ways of expressing what has occurred. In the **Magnificat,** all of the instances we have cited in the previous paragraph are of the Perfect Tense. That is, they express something that has been completed or perfected in the past. The Imperfect Tense expresses something that was going on, and there are other varieties as well. But, thanks to the fact that the **Magnificat** employs exclusively the Perfect Tense, we will concentrate on that.

Exsultavit, respexit, fecit, dispersit, deposuit, exaltavit, implevit, dimisit, locutus est. We must first sort these into kinds of verb or, as it is usually put, distinguish them according to the different conjugations to which they belong. We have already spoken of A-verbs and E-verbs. These are, respectfully, First Conjugation verbs and Third Conjugation verbs. In the Magnificat, A-verbs used in the perfect tense are **exsultare,** to rejoice or *to exult,* and **exaltare,** *to raise* or *to lift up.*

First Conjugation

The examples of verbs of this kind that we have already encountered are, **dare, inducare, liberare, sanctificare,** and **orare.** Here is the the Present Tense of First Conjugation or A-verbs.

Present Tense

Singular	*Plural*
1. **exsulto,** *I rejoice*	**exsultamus,** *we rejoice*
2. **exsultas,** *you rejoice*	**exsultatis,** *you rejoice*
3. **exsultat,** *he or she rejoices*	**exsultant,** *they rejoice*

The time-honored way to sum up one's knowledge of a Latin verb is to give its principal parts. What is the Latin verb meaning to love? Amo, amare, amavi, amatus. The analogous response in the case of to rejoice would be: **exsulto, exsultare, exsultavi, exsultatus.** The principal parts of the verb are: the first person singular of the present tense, the infinitive, the perfect and the past participle. Thus, putting the principal parts into English, we would have for **amare:** I love, to love, I loved, having loved. And for **exsultare:** I rejoice, to rejoice, I rejoiced, having rejoiced. Knowing the principal parts of a verb enables us quickly to formulate its various tenses. And, for our present purposes, it is especially convenient that the third principal part of any verb is precisely its perfect tense.

Perfect Tense

Singular	*Plural*
1. **exsultavi,** *I rejoiced*	**exsultavimus,** *we rejoiced*
2. **exsultavisti,** *you rejoiced*	**exsultavistis,** *you rejoiced*
3. **exsultavit,** *he or she rejoiced*	**exsultaverunt,** *they rejoiced*

The principal parts of **exaltare** are **exalto, exaltare, exaltavi, exaltatus.** Thus, the first person singular of the perfect tense is **exaltavi,** and you now know how to conjugate it in that tense: it follows exactly the pattern of **exultavi.**

Second Conjugation

One of the verbs in the **Magnificat** falls into the Second Conjugation, namely, **implevit.** The principal parts of this verb are: **impleo, implere, implevi, impletus:** *I fill up, to fill up, I filled up, having filled up.* Since the first principal part of a verb is the first person singular of its present tense, we may wonder how the present tense in this Second Conjugation is formed.

Present Tense

Singular	Plural
1. **impleo,** *I fill up*	**implemus,** *we fill up*
2. **imples,** *you fill up*	**impletis,** *you fill up*
3. **implet,** *he or she fills up*	**implent,** *they fill up*

And, given the third principal part of **implere,** we can build up its perfect tense.

Perfect Tense

Singular	Plural
1. **implevi,** *I filled up*	**implevimus,** *we filled up*
2. **implevisti,** *you filled up*	**implevistis,** *you filled up*
3. **implevit,** *he, she, or it filled up*	**impleverunt,** *they filled up*

Notice that the perfect tense of the First and Second Conjugations employ the same endings. To know how to conjugate the perfect tense of the one, given the third principal part of a verb, is to know how to conjugate the perfect tense of the other.

Third Conjugation

Five of the verbs used in the perfect tense in the **Magnificat** fall to the Third Conjugation, namely, **respexit, dispersit, deposuit, dimisit, fecit.** A glance suffices to tell us that these look very different from one another and indeed the Third Conjugation is a very commodious one, permitting a number of ways of forming the perfect tense. This would be confusing if we were not guided by the principal parts of these verbs, the third principal part being the first person singular of the perfect tense. So let us begin with their principal parts.

facio, facere, feci, factus
respicio, respicere, respexi, respectus
dispergo, dispergere, dispersi, dispersus
depono, deponere, deposui, depositus
dimitto, dimittere, dimisi, dimissus

The last is an old friend, familiar from the **Pater Noster**, where it appeared in the forms of **dimitte** and **dimittimus**. The former is the imperative, the latter the third person plural of the present tense. There we translated it as forgive, in the sense of set or put aside. In the **Magnificat**, the word means he put away or sent away.

Present Tense

Singular	*Plural*
1. **dimitto,** *I send away*	**dimittimus,** *we send away*
2. **dimittis,** *you send away*	**dimittitis,** *you send away*
3. **dimittit,** *she sends away*	**dimittunt,** *they send away*

In order to form its perfect tense, we consider the third principal part, namely, **dimisi**, which is the first person singular of the perfect tense.

Perfect Tense

Singular	*Plural*
1. **dimisi,** *I sent away*	**dimisimus,** *we sent away*
2. **dimisisti,** *you sent away*	**dimisistis,** *you sent away*
3. **dimisit,** *he sent away*	**dimiserunt,** *they sent away*

Thus, in the **Magnificat**, when we come upon line 14, **et divites dimisit inanes,** we know now that **dimisit** means *he sent away* and thus that the whole phrase means *the rich he has sent away empty*.

That leaves four verbs in the Third Conjugation **respexit, fecit, dispersit, deposuit.** They certainly look different from one another, but once we see their present and perfect tenses we will see why, despite differences, they are sufficiently alike to share the same Third Conjugation.

Present Tense of Facere, *to make or do*

Singular	Plural
1. facio	facimus
2. facis	facitis
3. facit	faciunt

There is no need, I hope, to indicate that these mean, in the singular, *I make or do, you make or do, he, she or it makes or does,* and in the plural, *we make or do, you make or do, they make or do.*

Perfect Tense of Facere, *to make or do*

Singular	Plural
1. feci	fecimus
2. fecisti	fecistis
3. fecit	fecerunt

These mean, or course, in the singular, *I made or did, you made or did, she, he, or it made or did,* and in the plural, *we made or did, you made or did, they made or did.*

Now we know precisely how the verb **fecit** is being used in the **Magnificat** when we read line 9. *Fecit potentiam in brachio suo.* **Fecit** is the third person singular of the perfect tense of **facere,** whose implied subject in line 6 is **Dominus,** *the Lord whom Mary is praising.*

Present Tense of Respicere

Singular	Plural
1. respicio	respicimus
2. respicis	respicitis
3. respicit	respiciunt

Perfect Tense of Respicere

Singular	Plural
1. respexi	respeximus
2. respexisti	respexistis
3. respexit	respexerunt

Thus when we read line 3 of the **Magnificat,** *quia respexit humiltatem ancillae suae,* we know that we have a third person singular of the perfect tense of **respicere** and that the Lord is being praised because he regarded the humility of his handmaid

Present Tense of Dispergere

The principal parts of this verb we remember are **dispergo, dispergere, dispersi, dispersus.** Thus its present tense is

Singular	*Plural*
1. **dispergo**	**dispergimus**
2. **dispergis**	**dispergitis**
3. **dispergit**	**dispergunt**

Its perfect tense will be formed from the first person singular, that is, from its third principal part, **dispersi.**

Perfect Tense of Dispergere

Singular	*Plural*
1. **dispersi**	**dispersimus**
2. **dispersisti**	**dispersistis**
3. **dispersit**	**disperserunt**

So when we read in the **Magnificat** *dispersit superbos*, we know that we are confronted by the third person singular of the perfect tense: *he sent away* or *dismissed the proud*. And when we read **deposuit potentes de sede,** we know that **deposuit** is the third person signular of the perfect tense of the verb whose principal parts are **depono, deponere, deposui, depositus.**

There is still another verb in the **Magnificat** we must take note of. It occurs in the line, **sicut locutus est ad patres nostros.** The principal parts of the verb of which this is a form are **loquor, loqui, locutus sum**. Odd. This is called a deponent verb, but all we want to notice now is that its perfect tense is composite.

Perfect Passive Form

Singular	*Plural*
1. **locutus sum**	**locuti sumus**
2. **locutus es**	**locuti estis**
3. **locutus est**	**locuti sunt**

That suffices to identify **locutus est** and explain why we translate the phrase: *as he spoke to our fathers.*

An added advantage of making this point is that it puts before us the present tense of the verb to be. The principal parts of that verb are **sum, esse, fui, futurus.** This is an irregular verb, hence that odd fourth principal part, The conjugation of the perfect tense of **esse** is:

	Singular	*Plural*
1.	**fui,** *I was*	**fuimus,** *we were*
2.	**fuisti,** *you were*	**fuistis,** *you were*
3.	**fuit,** *he, she, it was*	**fuerunt,** *they were*

Nouns

The **Magnificat** thus provides a rich source of knowledge of the perfect tenses of various conjugations of verbs. That is not its purpose, of course, but then your purpose is not to learn about verbs as a terminal objective either but rather, equipped with this knowledge, to be able to pray more completely Mary's beautiful expression of grateful praise because she had been chosen to be the mother of the Incarnate God and to be a principal instrument in the fulfillment of the prophecies that had sustained her people through the centuries. Now, as it happens, the **Magnificat** also provides an occasion to acquire knowledge of more Latin nouns.

The first one that occurs is **anima,** and we can use it to set forth the paradigm of the first kind of inflections of Latin nouns.

First Declension (-ae)

	Singular	Plural
Nominative	**anima**	**animae**
Genitive	**animae**	**animarum**
Dative	**animae**	**animis** (or **animabus**)
Accusative	**animam**	**animas**
Ablative	**anima**	**animis** (or **animabus**)

The way to identify the declension to which a noun belongs is by noticing its stem and genitive singular form. As we have just seen, **animae** is the genitive singular of the word for soul. Nouns of the first declension, accordingly, are called **-ae** nouns.

Other nouns in the **Magnificat** which belong to the first declension are: **ancilla, misericordia** and **potentia.**

Second Declension (-i)

The nouns of this declension are recognized by the fact that their genitive singular ends with *i*. In the **Magnificat,** an instance of this is **Deus,** not an ideal instance to illustrate the plural of such nouns. So let us take **Dominus.**

	Singular	*Plural*
Nominative	dominus	domini
Genitive	domini	dominorum
Dative	domino	dominis
Accusative	dominum	dominos
Ablative	domino	dominis

Another instance of such a noun in the **Magnificat** is **puer,** whose nominative singular is unusual but after that looks exactly like **dominus: puer, pueri, puero, puerum, puero** and, in the plural, **pueri, puerorum, pueris, pueros, pueris.** The word means *boy* or *son.* The Third Declension can be illustrated by **pater.**

Third Declension (-is)

	Singular	*Plural*
Nominative	pater	patres
Genitive	patris	patrum
Dative	patri	patribus
Accusative	patrem	patres
Ablative	patre	patribus

I think you will agree that that is enough abstract grammar for a while. But the point of this has not been to set forth the paradigms—you will find them displayed in the grammatical appendix to this book but to enable you to go through the **Magnificat** and identify the words according to the roles they play. Since Latin is an inflected language; we discover how nouns work by noticing their endings. If a noun is singular or accusative, say, knowing this will determine whether we understand the passage in which it occurs. Now some of the nouns in the **Magnificat** are fourth (**-us**) and fifth (**-ei**) declension nouns, e.g., **spiritus** and **progenies,** respectfully, and we will come back to that.

Here is an exercise you can undertake now. Go back to the text of the **Magnificat** at the beginning of this lesson and make lists of all the nouns and verbs that occur in the text. You can make a separate list for adjectives and another for prepositions. We have not covered enough yet for you to do this in the confidence that your lists will be exhaustive or that you will not put a verb in your noun column and vice versa. Nonetheless, the exercise is important. Only by knowing the cases and tenses of verbs can we understand a Latin passage. But this exercise, by concentrating on one of the prayers you want to grasp in the Latin, makes all this otherwise abstract grammar subservient to your main objective. The comprehensive vocabulary at the end of this book identifies all regular nouns and verbs by their declensions and conjugations, respectively, and the grammatical appendix gives the declensions and conjugations, so you can check your work easily.

The term used to signify this activity is *parsing*. Perhaps you took Latin in school and remember being called upon to recite. You would read the passage, give a translation and then be asked to parse particular words in it. Or perhaps you are starting utterly from scratch. In either case, you will want to be able to parse the words in the text. Which of course you can now do, at least in part. You are asked to parse **exsultavit,** and you say, "That is the third person singular of the perfect tense of **exsultare.**" Similarly, asked about **fecit,** you reply, "Why, that is the third person singular of the perfect tense of **facere.**"

Lesson Four

Symbolum Apostolorum

The Apostles Creed

1. **Credo in Deum,**
2. **Patrem omnipotentem,**
3. **Creatorem caeli et terrae.**
4. **Et in Jesum Christum,**
5. **Filium ejus unicum,**
6. **Dominum nostrum:**
7. **qui conceptus est de Spiritu Sancto,**
8. **natus ex Maria Virgine,**
9. **passus sub Pontio Pilato,**
10. **crucifixus, mortuus, et sepultus,**
11. **descendit ad inferos;**
12. **tertia die resurrexit a mortuis**
13. **ascendit ad caelos;**
14. **sedet ad dexteram Dei Patris omnipotentis:**
15. **inde venturus est judicare vivos et mortuos.**
16. **Credo in Spiritum Sanctum,**
17. **sanctam Ecclesiam catholicam,**
18. **Sanctorum communionem,**
19. **remissionem peccatorum,**
20. **carnis resurrectionem,**
21. **vitam aeternam. Amen.**

[1] I believe in God
[2] the Father almighty
[3] creator of heaven and earth.
[4] and in Jesus Christ
[5] his only son
[6] our Lord
[7] who was conceived by the Holy Spirit
[8] born of the Virgin Mary
[9] suffered under Pontius Pilate,

[10] was crucified, died and was buried,
[11] he descended into hell
[12] on the third day he rose from the dead
[13] ascended into heaven
[14] he is seated at the right hand of God the almighty Father
[15] whence he will come to judge the living and the dead.
[16] I believe in the Holy Spirit
[17] the holy Catholic Church
[18] the communion of saints,
[19] the forgiveness of sins,
[20] the resurrection of the body
[21] and life everlasting. Amen.

Since you now know the Pater Noster and **Ave Maria,** you will be able to pray the Rosary in Latin when you know the **Symbolum Apostolorum,** or Apostle's Creed, and the doxology: **Gloria Patri, et Filio et Spiritui Sancto, sicut erat in principio, et nunc et semper et in saecula saeculorum. Amen.** Of course you will also want to know the Latin for the fifteen mysteries on which we meditate while saying the rosary. All that will be done in this lesson. But first the Creed.

1. God the Father

Since this is a profession of faith, the key verb is credo, *I believe.* Everything from lines 1 to 15 is governed by the first occurrence of the verb, and everything from 16 through 21 is governed by the reiteration of **credo.** The objects of the profession of faith are introduced by the preposition **in** followed by an accusative.

Thus, **Credo in Deum, Patrem omnipotentem, Creatorem caeli et terrae.** God is the primary object of faith, so the accusative of **deus** follows immediately after the **in.** And who is God? The Father almighty. **Patrem,** we know, is the accusative of **pater,** and is said to be in apposition to **Deum.** That is why it agrees with it in gender, num- ber, and case, much as an adjective would, and indeed as the adjective **omnipotentem**—the accusative of **omnipotens**—agrees with its noun, **Patrem.** This is carried on as the God in whom one is professing belief is acknowledged also as the creator of heaven and earth. **Creatorem** is the singular accusative of **creator** and **caeli** and **terrae** are genitives, the former of **caelum,** a noun with which we are familiar from our study of the **Pater Noster,** and the latter of **terra.**

To which declensions do **deus, pater, creator, caelum** and **terra** belong? When you have correctly identified them, decline them in both the singular and plural. You can check your work by consulting the vocabulary at the end of the book.

2. God the Son

The profession of faith continues—Et in Jesum Christum: *and in Jesus Christ*. Both *Jesus* and *Christ* are in the accusative case as objects of the verb credo as followed by **in**.

Two things are now said of Christ: that he is the unique Son of the Father and our Lord. That is, **Filium ejus unicum**. Both the second declension noun **Filium** and its adjective **unicum** are in the accusative case. Whose son? His, that is, God the Father's = **ejus**. The nominative of that is **is, ea, id** in the masculine, feminine, and neuter: *he, she, it*. The genitive of all of these, despite their differences in gender, is **eius** or **ejus**.

Dominum nostrum, *Our Lord*—again the noun and its adjective are both in the accusative, since they are governed by the original **Credo in.**

With the introduction of the relative pronoun **qui** = *who*, we can switch back into the nominative case since what follows is taken to modify the *he* in the implied *he who*. Thus, we find a suite of phrases descriptive of Jesus, no longer in the accusative, but as agreeing with the *he* implied in the relative pronoun **qui**.

* **qui conceptus est de Spiritu Sancto**—we could render this as *who conceived is of the Holy Spirit* and thereby reveal our neophyte status. **Conceptus est** is a compound past tense, the perfect, formed of the participle of the verb **concipere**, whose principal parts are **concipio, concipere, concepi, conceptum**. That fourth principal part is precisely the past participle of the word: *having been conceived*.

* **de** is a preposition governing the ablative case, **spiritu** is the ablative of the fourth declension noun **spiritus**, whereas **sancto** is an ablative of the adjective exhibiting the form of the second declension.

Fourth Declension

	Singular	Plural
Nominative	manus	manus
Genitive	manus	manuum
Dative	manui	manibus
Accusative	manum	manus
Ablative	manu	manibus

* **natus ex Maria Virgine**—*born of the Virgin Mary.* Being born is something that happened to the Son; He was born. If the verb were spelled out here, it would be **natus est.** This, like **conceptus est,** is a passive past tense. Unlike it however, **natus est** is the only participle the verb **nascor** has, a verb which is only passive in form: *to be born.* Its principal parts are **nascor, nasci, natus sum,** all passive forms.

* **passus sub Pontio Pilato**—*under Pontius Pilate,* that is, under his jurisdiction. **Sub** is a preposition which governs the ablative case, and both proper names are ablatives of the second declension. **Passus** like **natus** is the participle of a verb which exists only in the passive form. The principal parts are **patior, pati, passus sum.** This verb means to suffer, which of course is always something that happens to the sufferer, that is, it is always a passive verb.

* **crucifixus, mortuus et sepultus,** that is, **crucifixus est, mortuus est, sepultus est,** passive participles which modify the *he* in *he who* and thus are in the nominative case, all of them exhibiting the perfect passive of the second declension.

* **descendit ad inferos**—this active verb has the implied **is** or **ille,** *he,* in **qui** for its subject; **descendit** is the third person singular perfect tense of **descendere,** a third conjugation verb. **Inferos** is an accusative plural governed by the preposition **ad.**

* **tertia die resurrexit a mortuis.** There are several interesting things, **grammatice loquendo,** in this phrase. First of all **tertia die.** Knowing the Creed, you know that this means *on the third day.* How does Latin express that? You might think that **tertia** is a nominative case. But it is an ablative of the first declension **tertius, -a, -um,** just as **die** is the ablative of the fifth declension noun **dies.** The two form a little ablative phrase expressive of time when—on the third day.

Fifth Declension

	Singular	Plural
Nominative	dies	dies
Genitive	diei	dierum
Dative	diei	diebus
Accusative	diem	dies
Ablative	die	diebus

Resurrexit is the third person singular of the perfect tense of **resurgo, resurgere, resurrexi, resurrectus.** The preposition **a** (it would be **ab** if it were followed by a word beginning with a vowel rather than one beginning with a consonant) governs the ablative, and **mortuis** is an ablative plural in the second declension of the masculine of the adjective **mortuus, mortua, mortuum.**

* **ascendit ad caelos.** No problem here; **ascendit** is the third person singular of the perfect tense of **ascendo, ascendere, ascendi, ascensus,** a standard case of a third conjugation verb. **Caelos** is the accusative plural of **caelum** governed by the preposition **ad,** meaning *to* or *toward.*

* **sedet ad dexteram Dei Patris omnipotentis.** The tense of the second conjugation verb **sedere** is the present: Christ is seated at the right hand of God the Father Almighty. **Ad dexteram,** *at the right,* calls for the genitives of **deus, Pater,** and **omnipotens.**

* **inde venturus est judicare vivos et mortuos.** The adverb **inde** *thence, from there, from that place,* introduces a future participle of the verb **venio.** The following construction is similar to the English: *he will come to judge,* with the simple infinitive employed, **judicare.** Latin has more complicated and nuanced ways of expressing such an action, as indeed has English. *In order that he might judge.* But in both languages the infinitive suffices and is used here. The infinitive **judicare** takes the accusatives **vivos** and **mortuos.**

3. God the Holy Spirit

Credo in Spiritum Sanctum. Once more the verb **credo,** present tense first person singular, followed by **in,** takes an object in the accusative, and both the fourth declension noun **spiritum** and its adjective **sanctum** are accusatives.

* **sanctam Ecclesiam catholicam:** here the noun is bracketed by two adjectives, and all three are in the accusative case, objects of **credo in.**

* **sanctorum communionem:** the noun here as the object of **credo in** is in the accusative case. And what is the community in which I believe? That of the saints. **Sanctorum,** you recognize, is the genitive plural of **sanctus.**

* **remissionem peccatorum:** again an accusative, the singular accusative of the noun **remissio** as the object of **credo. Re-mittere** is a compound verb whose literal meaning is to send back. The sending back or remission or forgiveness of what? Sins. Hence the genitive plural of our old friend, alas, **peccatum.**

* **carnis resurrectionem:** this noun is formed from **resurgere** and is accusative as the object of **credo in:** the rising or resurrecting . . . of what? The flesh. **Carnis** is the genitive of **caro.**

* **vitam aeternam:** finally the believer says, "I believe in life everlasting." Two accusatives, therefore. And then **Amen.**

The Rosary

Quinque mysteria gaudiosa
1. **Annuntiatio angeli Mariae**
   Pater noster
   Ave Maria (*decies*)[1]
   Gloria Patri . . .
2. **Visitatio**
   Pater noster
   Ave Maria (*decies*)
   Gloria Patri . . .
3. **Incarnatio Domini nostri Jesu Christi**
   Pater noster
   Ave Maria (*decies*)
   Gloria patri . . .
4. **Presentatio Jesu in templo**
   Pater noster

---

1   Day-chee-ez = ten times.

Ave Maria (*decies*)
Gloria patri . . .
5. Inventio pueri Jesu in templo
Pater noster
Ave Maria (*decies*)
Gloria patri . . .

Quinque mysteria dolorosa
1. **Agonia in hortu**
Pater noster
Ave Maria (*decies*)
Gloria patri . . .
2. **Flagellatio Jesu**
Pater noster
Ave maria (*decies*)
Gloria patri . . .
3. **Coronatio spinis**
Pater noster
Ave Maria (*decies*)
Gloria patri . . .
4. **Via dolorosa**
Pater noster
Ave Maria (*decies*)
Gloria patri . . .
5. **Crucifixio Iesu**
Pater noster
Ave Maria (*decies*)
Gloria patri . . .

Quinque mysteria gloriosa
1. **Resurrectio Iesu**
Pater noster
Ave Maria (*decies*)
Gloria patri . . .
2. **Ascensio Iesu**
Pater noster
Ave Maria (*decies*)
Gloria patri . . .
3. **Descensus spiritus sancti**
Pater noster
Ave Maria (*decies*)

Gloria patri . . .
4. **Assumptio Beatae Virginis Mariae**
   Pater noster
   Ave Maria (*decies*)
   Gloria patri . . .
5. **Coronatio Mariae Reginae coeli**
   Pater noster
   Ave Maria (*decies*)
   Gloria patri . . .

At Fatima, the angel taught the seers the following prayer, to be said after the **Gloria** ending each decade:

Miserere nobis, Jesu; libera nos ab ignibus inferi;
induca omnes animas in coelum,
maxime eos in maximo periculo.

Jesus, have mercy; deliver us from the fires of hell;
draw all souls to heaven,
especially those in greatest need.

Salve Regina

1. Salve, Regina, mater misericordiae;
   vita, dulcedo et spes nostra, salve.
2. Ad te clamamus exsules filii Hevae.
3. Ad te suspiramus gementes et flentes in hac lacrimarum
   valle.
4. Eja ergo, advocata nostra,
   illos tuos misericordes oculos ad nos converte.
5. Et Jesum, benedictum fructum ventris tui,
   nobis post hoc exilium ostende.
6. O clemens, o pia, o dulcis Virgo Maria.
7. Ora pro nobis, sancta Dei Genetrix.
8. Ut digni efficiamur promissionibus Christi.
9. Oremus. Omnipotens sempiterne Deus,
10. qui gloriosae Virginis Matris Mariae corpus et animam,
11. ut dignum Filii tui habitaculum effici mereretur,
12. Spiritu Sancto cooperante, praeparasti:
13. da, ut cujus commemoratione laetamur;
14. pia intercessione, ab instantibus malis,
15. et a morte perpetua liberemur.
16. Per eundem Christum Dominum nostrum. Amen.

1. **Salve, Regina, mater misericordiae**

Salve—an imperative of the second conjugation verb **salvere,** *to be in good health, to be well.* In this form, it has the meaning of *Hail* or *May it be well with you.* The noun **mater** is in apposition to **Regina;** both are in the vocative, as are **nostra vita, nostra dulcedo, nostra spes. Spes** is a fifth declension noun, following the pattern of **dies.**

Fifth Declension

	Singular	Plural
Nominative	dies	diei
Genitive	diei	dierum
Dative	diei	diebus

Accusative	diem	dies
Ablative	die	diebus
Vocative	dies	dies

* vita, dulcedo et spes nostra, salve

Dulcedo, dulcedinis is a feminine noun of the third declension; **vita, -ae,** (1), *life,* and **spes, -ei,** f. (5), *hope. Hail [Holy] Queen, Mother of Mercy; our life, our sweetness and our hope, hail.*

2. Ad te clamamus exsules filii Hevae.

Filii, the nominative plural of **filius** is the subject of the verb, meaning here, *children* and not simply sons. **Exules** is also a noun: it is nominative plural of **exul, exulis.** Here it has adjectival force: *banished children,* **Hevae,** *of Eve.* The verb **clamamus** gives no trouble: a first person plural of the present tense of the first conjugation verb **clamare,** *to cry out.* **Ad te** = *to you. To you do we banished children of Eve cry out.*

3. Ad te suspiramus gementes et flentes in hac lacrimarum valle.

Suspiramus—*we sigh;* parsed as is **clamamus.** The subject of the verb is understood, we, and the subject is modified by two present participles in the nominative plural to agree with that understood *we.* **Gemo, gemere, gemui, gemitus,** *to groan, to mourn,* and **fleo, flere, flevi, fletus,** *to cry, give us,* **gementes** and **flentes:** *mourning and weeping.* Where? **In hac lacrimarum valle:** *in this vale of tears. To thee do we send up our sighs, mourning and weeping in this vale of tears.*

4. Eja ergo advocata nostra,

Eja is an interjection, meaning *well;* **ergo** = therefore; here, the two give us: *well, then.* **Advocata nostra** = vocatives, since we address Mary as our advocate.

* illos tuos misericordes oculos ad nos converte.

Converte is a deprecatory imperative from **convertere,** *to turn.* Turn what? **oculos tuos:** accusative plurals, of the noun **oculus, -i,** m., *eye,* and of the possessive adjective which agrees with the noun it modifies. **Illos,** *those,* is also accusative plural and modifying the noun **oculos.** *Those your eyes*—emphatic. **Misericordes** too modifies eyes: *those your merciful eyes.* **Ad nos**—*to or toward us. Turn then, our advocate, those your eyes of mercy toward us.*

5. **Et Jesum, benedictum fructum ventris tui, nobis post hoc exsilium ostende.**

Ostende, *show,* deprecatory imperative of **ostendere,** *to show,* is the verb that controls this sentence. Its direct object is **Jesum,** accusative of the proper name, *Jesus. Show Jesus,* to whom? **Nobis—** *to us,* dative plural. When? **Post hoc exsilium:** *after this exile.* **Post** is a preposition that takes the accusative: **exilium** is a neuter noun whose accusative is the same form as its nominative. **Benedictum fructum ventris tui** modifies **Jesum.** **Fructum** is a singular accusative of the fourth declension noun **fructus,** and it is modified by **benedictum,** which agrees with it; it means *blessed. Blessed fruit* **ventris tui,** *of thy womb. After this exile, show us the blessed fruit of thy womb, Jesus.*

6. **O clemens, o pia, o dulcis Virgo Maria.**

This sentence is vocative, as the repetition of **O** underscores. **Clemens, clementis,** mild, kind, merciful; **pia,** the feminine of **pius, pia, pium,** *dutiful, pious;* **dulcis,** *sweet*—all feminine adjectives modifying **Virgo,** from **virgo, virginis,** *virgin.* And **Maria** is in apposition to **Virgo.**

7. **Ora pro nobis, sancta Dei Genetrix.**

Versicle. **Ora,** the singular imperative of **orare. Dei genetrix**—*O holy parent or mother of God:* this is Mary's most awesome title.

8. **Ut digni efficiamur promissionibus Christi.**

Response. **Efficiamur** is the first person plural of the subjunctive passive of **efficere,** *to effect or bring about;* the subjunctive introduced by **ut,** *that, in order that.* The meaning is: *that we might be made.* What? **Digni,** *worthy,* nominative plural, to answer to *we.* Of what? **Promissionibus Christi:** the ablative follows on *worthy—worthy as to the promises of Christ. That we might be made worthy of the promises of Christ.*

9. **Oremus. Omnipotens, sempiterne Deus,**

Oremus is first person plural of the present subjunctive of **orare:** *let us pray.* Why **sempiterne?** The adjective is **sempiternus, sempiterna, sempiternum,** in the masculine, feminine, and neuter, respectively. **Omnipotens,** all mighty—**omnis potens**—modifies **Deus.** Of course, you know the answer. The vocative singular of the second declension ends in *e.*

10. **qui gloriosae Virginis Matris Mariae corpus et animam,**

The verb controlling lines 10, 11, and 12 is **praeparasti,** the second person singular of the perfect active of **preparare:** the whole is introduced by the relative pronoun, **qui,** and since we are addressing Almighty God, it is translated, *you who prepared;* **corpus et animam,** two singular accusatives, direct objects, **corpus, corporis,** and **anima, animae**—*body and soul.* Whose? **Gloriosae Virginis Matris, Mariae**—all genitives, of course. Of the glorious Virgin Mother, Mary.

11. **ut dignum Filii tui habitaculum effici mereretur,**

Prepared for what reason? **Ut** = *in order that;* this calls for a subjunctive verb. Where is it? **Mereretur**—third person subjunctive passive of the second conjugation verb **merere,** *to be worthy, that she might be made worthy.* Of what? **Effici**—this is the passive subjunctive infinitive of **efficere,** a fourth conjugation verb. *That she might be made worthy,* or literally, *that she might be made worthy to become.* What? **Habitaculum**—*a dwelling place.* Whose? **Filii tui:** *of your son.* **Dignum** modifies *dwelling place: that she might become a worthy dwelling place of your Son.*

12. **Spiritu cooperante, praeparasti:**

Now an ablative absolute—**Spiritu** is an ablative and is modified by the adjective in the ablative case, the two joined with the ablative singular of the present participle of the deponent verb, **operor,** to work, **co-operor,** *to work with.* So the phrase has the meaning: *the Holy Spirit working with you.* So the thought is Trinitarian: the Father prepares a dwelling place for the Son with the cooperation of the Holy Spirit.

13. **da, ut cujus commemoratione laetamur;**

We are familiar with the imperative of **dare:** *give, grant.* Grant what? **Ut,** *that* **laetamur.** First person plural, indicative, but passive in form. Because **laetor** is a deponent verb meaning that, while passive in form, it is active in meaning. *Grant that we who rejoice or are made glad* **commemoratione,** *by the commemoration* **cujus,** *of who, of whom, of Mary.*

14. **pia intercessione, ab instantibus malis,**

Liberemur at the end of line 15 controls the thought; it is governed by the previous **ut** and is a first person plural subjunctive passive of **liberare:** that we might be freed. How? **pia interces-sione,** *by intercession.* What kind? **pia** *upright, virtuous: her* is under-stood here: *by her pious intercession.* Saved from what? **Ab instantibus malis,** *from evils,* but what kind? *Instantibus*—an abla-tive plural of a present participle of **instare. Stare** means *to stand,* **instare** means *to stand around, to be present. May we be freed by her pious intercession from present or pressing evils.*

15. et a morte perpetua liberemur.

Freed too **a morte,** *from death.* Death? But all men are mortal. **A morte perpetua**—*lasting death, from being cut off forever from a share in the life of God.*

16. Per eundem Christum Dominum nostrum, Amen.

Our prayer is addressed to God through our mediator, already mentioned in the prayer, hence through **eundem,** accusative sin-gular, the same Jesus Christ. All these accusatives are governed of course by the preposition **per,** including **Dominum nostrum,** our Lord.

Hymnus Ambrosianus

Te Deum Laudamus

1. Te Deum laudamus, te Dominum confitemur.
2. Te aeternum Patrem omnis terra veneratur.
3. Tibi omnes Angeli, tibi Caeli, et universae Potestates:
4. Tibi Cherubim et Seraphim incessabili voce proclamant:
5. Sanctus, Sanctus, Sanctus, Dominus Deus Sabaoth.
6. Pleni sunt caeli et terra majestatis gloriae tuae.
7. Te gloriosus Apostolorum chorus,
8. Te Prophetarum laudabilis numerus,
9. Te Martyrum candidatus laudat exercitus.
10. Te per orbem terrarum sancta confitetur Ecclesia,
11. Patrem immensae majestatis;
12. Venerandum tuum verum et unicum Filium;
13. Sanctum quoque Paraclitum Spiritum.
14. Tu Rex gloriae, Christe.
15. Tu Patris sempiternus es Filius.
16. Tu, ad liberandum suscepturus hominem, non horruisti Virginis uterum.
17. Tu, devicto mortis aculeo, aperuisti credentibus regna caelorum.
18. Tu ad dexteram Dei sedes, in gloria Patris.
19. Judex crederis esse venturus.
20. Te ergo quaesumus, tuis famulis subveni, quos pretioso sanguine redemisti.
21. Aeterna fac cum Sanctis tuis in gloria numerari.
22. Salvum fac populum tuum, Domine, et benedic hereditati tuae.
23. Et rege eos, et extolle illos usque in aeternum.
24. Per singulos dies benedicimus te;
25. Et laudamus nomen tuum in saeculum, et in saeculum saeculi.
26. Dignare, Domine, die isto sine peccato nos custodire.

27. **Miserere nostri, Domine, miserere nostri.**
28. **Fiat misericordia tua, Domine, super nos, quemad-modum speravimus in te.**
29. **In te, Domine, speravi: non confundar in aeternum.**

1. **Te Deum laudamus, te Dominum confitemur.**

This great prayer of praise is dominated by the recurrence of **te,** the personal pronoun, usually in the accusative case, sometimes in the dative, **tibi. Te Deum Laudamus**—*thee God we praise.* The verb is a first person plural of the present active of the first conjugation verb, **laudare.** The thought is continued: *thee Lord* **confitemur:** from the deponent **confiteor:** *we confess.*

2. **Te aeternam Patrem omnis terra veneratur.**

The subject here is **omnis terra,** *the whole earth.* The verb is **veneratur**—again a deponent, so this has the active sense of venerates. *The whole earth venerates* **te aeternum Patrem,** *thee, eternal Father.*

3. **Tibi omnes Angeli, tibi Caeli, et universae Potestates:**

Tibi, the dative, *to thee,* in this line and in the next, is controlled by the verb at the end of 4, **proclamant:** *they proclaim to thee.* Who does? **Omnes angeli, caeli, universae potestates**—*all the angels, the heavens, all the powers.* For example? Next line.

4. **Tibi Cherubim et Seraphim incessabili voce proclamant:**

Cherubim and Seraphim. All these proclaim **incessabili voce**—*with unceasing voice.* That is, of course, the ablative of both noun, **voc, vocis,** f. (3) and adjective, **incessabilis.**

5. **Sanctus, Sanctus, Sanctus, Dominus Deus Sabaoth.**

And now what seems almost a reflective pause in the outburst of praise. The repetition of **Sanctus** slowing down the recitation: *holy, holy, holy.* **Dominus Deus Sabaoth:** *Lord God of Sabaoth.*

6. **Pleni sunt caeli et terra majestatis gloriae tuae.**

The subject is the compound **caeli et terra,** *the heavens and the earth,* **pleni sunt,** *are full:* the adjective in the plural, to accommodate the complex subject and/or to agree with **caeli.** What are the heavens and the earth full of? **Majestatis gloriae tuae:** *of the majesty of your glory.* A double genitive.

7. Te gloriosus Apostolorum chorus,

A return now to the original motif. Lines 7, 8, and 9 share the verb expressed in 9, **laudat**. It has three subjects: **chorus** in 7, **numerus** in 8, **exercitus** in 9. **Gloriosus** modifies **chorus**: *the glorious choir* **Apostolorum**, *of apostles* (praises) **te**: *thee.*

8. Te Prophetarum laudabilis numerus,

Laudabilis modifies **numerus**: *the laudable number* **Prophetarum**, *of prophets* (praises) *you.*

9. Te Martyrum candidatus laudat exercitus.

Candidatus modifies **exercitus**, *army.* What kind of army? The adjective means *shining, white:* it is the past participle of **candere**, *to shine, to glitter.* So: *the gleaming army* **Martyrum**, *of martyrs,* **laudat te**, *praises you.*

10. Te per orbem terrarum sancta confitetur Ecclesia.

Ecclesia is the subject and has the adjective **sancta**: *holy Church* **confitetur te**, *confesses you*—remember that **confiteor** is a deponent verb—confesses where? **Per orbem terrarum**—*throughout the orb of the lands,* literally: *throughout the world.*

11. Patrem immensae majestatis;

Patrem is in apposition to **te**, *thee, Father,* **immensae majestatis**: *of immense majesty.*

12. Venerandum tuum verum et unicum Filium;

Venerandum, with **sit** understood, is a gerund formed from **venerare**: it carries the note of oughtness or obligation or necessity. Its subject is **filium** which is modified by **tuum verum unicum**—*your true unique Son.* Why the accusative? Because the Son, like the Father in line 11, is the object of the confessing of the Church mentioned in 10. The Church confesses your true and unique Son, *who ought to be venerated*: and now we see why **venerandum** and not **venerandus**. The gerundive agrees with **filium** in gender, number, and case: it is a verbal adjective.

13. Sanctum quoque Paraclitum Spiritum.

Spiritum sanctum, *the holy Spirit,* is also confessed by the Church throughout the world—**quoque** = *also*—the Holy Spirit who is the **Paraclitum**, *the Paraclite.*

14. Tu Rex gloriae, Christe.

We switch from the accusative to the vocative: **tu,** *thou,* and the addressee is **Christe,** also in the vocative, **rex gloriae:** *king of glory.*

15. Tu Patris sempiternus es Filius.

Here we have the verb that controls lines 14 and 15, **es,** second person singular of **esse:** *Thou, Christ, are* **filius** *the son of the Father,* the **sempiternus,** *eternal Son, as well as the king of glory.*

16. Tu, ad liberandum suscepturus hominem, non horruisti Virginis uterum.

We continue to address Christ, and a lengthy thought begins. **Ad liberandum hominem,** *in order to liberate man,* **suscepturus:** *took upon yourself. You undertook to liberate man;* **non horruisti:** perfect tense, second person singular of **horrere** (2): *you did not disdain* **uterum, uterus, -i,** m.—*the womb,* **Virginis,** *of the Virgin.*

17. Tu, devicto mortis aculeo, aperuisti credentibus regna caelorum

Tu aperuisti—from **aperire,** *to open,* again second person sungular of the perfect active, *you opened,* **regna caelorum,** *the kingdom of heaven.* To whom? **Credentibus,** *to those believing, to believers.* **Devicto** is from **devinco, devincere, devici, devictus,** *to conquer;* **aculeus,** a second declension noun meaning *sting.* Both the noun and its modifier, **devicto,** are ablatives = *having conquered the sting of death, you opened the kingdom of heaven to believers.*

18. Tu ad dexteram Dei sedes, in gloria Patris.

Sedes, from **sedere** (2), is the verb: *you sit* **ad dexteram,** *at the right, at the right hand of,* **Dei,** *of God,* **in gloria Patris,** *in the glory of the Father.*

19. Judex crederis esse venturus.

Crederis: *you are believed to be,* **judex,** *the judge,* **venturus,** *who is to come.*

20. Te ergo quaesumus, tuis famulis subveni, quos pretioso sanguine redemisti.

Quaesumus—*we beseech* **te,** *you,* **ergo,** *therefore,* **subveni,** *to assist*—taking the dative: **tuis famulis,** *your servants,* **quos,** *whom,* **redemisti,** second person singular perfect tense, *have redeemed.*

How? **Sanguine,** ablative of **sanguis, sanguinis,** masculine, modified by the adjective **pretioso,** also accordingly in the ablative singular: *by precious blood. We beseech you therefore to assist your servants whom you have redeemed with (your) precious blood.*

21. Aeterna fac cum Sanctis tuis in glora numerari.

Numerari, passive infinite = *to be numbered,* **cum sanctis tuis,** *with your saints,* in **gloria aeterna,** *in eternal glory.* All this is governed by the imperative of **facere, fac**—*make* (them) *to be numbered among your holy ones in eternal glory.*

22. Salvum fac populum tuum, Domine, et benedic hereditati tuae.

Salvum fac —*make safe or saved,* or, simply, *save,* **populum tuum,** *your people,* **Domine,** *Lord;* and then another imperative, this one from **benedicere: benedic,** *bless,* taking the dative: **haereditati tuae,** *your inheritance.*

23. Et rege eos, et extolle illos usque in aeternum.

Et rege eos: regere is a third conjugation verb, **rego, regere, rexi, rectus,** *to rule;* so: *and rule them,* this verb taking the accusative, **eos;** and then another imperative, **extolle,** this from **ex + tollo, tollere, sustuli, sublatus,** an irregular verb of the third conjugation, which even without the prefix means *to raise up, to elevate;* so: *raise them up* in **aeternum,** *to eternity, to the eternal, forever.*

24. Per singulos dies benedicimus te;

Benedicimus: the prayer shifts back to the creatures praying: *we bless you.* When? **Per singulos dies. Dies, diei,** a fifth declension noun, is here taken as masculine (it sometimes is feminine), and the form is the accusative plural; this can be seen from its adjective, **singulos,** a nice solid accusative plural of the second declension, meaning *single, or each:* here, **per singulos dies,** *through every day,* literally, or simply, *every day: We bless you every day, daily.*

25. Et laudamus nomen tuum in saeculum, et in saeculum saeculi.

Et laudamus—the pledge continues: *we praise* **nomen tuum,** *your name,* in **saeculum,** *into an age, for an age;* and then more emphastically, **et in saeculum saeculi,** *for the age of an age, for ages, forever. And we praise thy name forever.*

26. Dignare, Domine, die isto sine peccato nos custodire.

And now a petition. **Dignare:** this is the imperative of the deponent verb in the first conjugation, **dignor,** to esteem or honor, to deem, or *deign. Deign, Lord, this day*—**die isto,** an ablative of duration, when or how long, **custodire:** this is an infinitive, following on the imperative **dignare:** *deign to keep* **nos,** *us,* **sine peccato,** *without sin, sinless. Deign, Lord, to keep us sinless this day.*

27. Miserere nostri, Domine, miserere nostri.

Miserere, the imperative from the deponent **misereor,** to have mercy, a deponent of the second conjugation, whose object is in the genitive. Thus this very familiar construction is odd both in verb and object: a passive imperative with an active sense and a direct object in the genitive. **Miserere nostri:** *have mercy on us,* **Domine.** And then the repetition. **Miserere nostri.**

28. Fiat misericordia tua, Domine, super nos, quemadmodum speravimus in te.

Misericordia tua—the thought is repeated, expressed differently. **Fiat,** *let be, may your mercy come to be* **super nos,** *upon us,* **Domine,** *Lord.* And then a very interesting compound, **quemadmodum = ad modum quem,** in the manner which or just as or, very simply, as: **speravimus,** a first person plural of the perfect active of **sperare:** *as we have hoped or put our trust,* **in te** = *in thee.*

29. In te, Domine, speravi: non confundar in aeternum.

And now, in the final line, an abrupt switch to the first person singular: **speravi:** *I have hoped* **in te,** *in thee,* **Domine; non confundar** = the first person singular of the present subjunctive of the third conjugation verb **confundo, confundere, confudi, confusus.** *May I not be confused?* The verb requires a far stronger sense here. To be thrown into disorder, in short, to be lost **in aeternum,** *forever. In thee, O Lord, have I hoped; may I not be eternally lost.*

At this point, having analyzed and parsed and broken into pieces this magnificent prayer, you should say it through in one fervent recitation, feeling its dramatic and rolling progression, its solemn profession of praise and trust and worship of God. This is the prayer for those great occasions when we are conscious of being blessed in some particular and unusual way. This was the prayer sung at the conclusion of war, at a coronation or other great public event or deliverance. Like all the prayers we have studied, it should be committed to memory so that it can spring spontaneously to our lips at the appropriate moment. In this way, the pedestrian parsing and analysis of its component words will have served its true purpose—not to give us an abstract knowledge of Latin grammar but to enable us to pray with understanding and devotion the great Latin prayers of the Church.

Psalm 31

THE PSALMS ARE AN ESSENTIAL PART of the prayer of the Church. From earliest times, the praying of the Psalter was part of the *opus Dei*, the work of God. In monasteries, in choir, monks chanted the canonical hours, each of which consisted of a number of psalms. Secular priests recited the office as contained in the *Breviarium Romanum* or in the manual edition appropriate to this religious order or that.

We shall analyze and parse three of the some 150 psalms. Relatively short ones have been chosen to facilitate memorization.

Psalm 31

1. Beatus cui remissa est iniquitas, * et obtectum est peccatum.
2. Beatus vir, cui non imputavit Dominus delictum, * nec est in spiritu eius dolus.
3. Quoniam tacui, inveteraverunt ossa mea * dum rugirem tota die.
4. Quoniam die ac nocte gravata erat super me manus tua, * immutatus est vigor meus in ardoribus aestatis.
5. Peccatum meum cognitum tibi feci, * et delictum meum non abscondi. Dixi: "Confitebor adversum me iniquitatem meam Domino," * et tu remisisti impietatem peccati mei.
6. Propter hoc orabit ad te omnis sanctus * in tempore opportuno. Et in diluvio aquarum multarum ad eum non approximabunt.
7. Tu es refugium meum, a tribulatione conservabis me; * exsultationibus salutis circumdabis me.
8. Intellectum tibi dabo et instruam te in via, qua gradieris; firmabo super te oculos meos.
9. Nolite fieri sicut equus et mulus, quibus non est intellec-

tus in camo et freno; et accedis ad constringendum, non
approximant ad te.

10. **Multi dolores impii; ***
sperantem autem in Domino misericordia circumdabit.

11. **Laetamini in Domino et exsultate, justi; ***
et gloriamini, omnes recti corde.

[1] Blessed is he whose wickedness is forgiven and whose sin
is covered.

[2] Blessed the man to whom the Lord does not impute
blame, nor is there guile in his spirit.

[3] As long as I was silent, my bones wasted away, while all
day long I groan.

[4] For day and night your hand was heavy upon me, my
strength was changed in the heat of summer.

[5] I have made known my sin to you, and have not hidden
my fault. I said, "I will confess my iniquity before you,"
and you forgave the impiety of my sin.

[6] Therefore every holy one will pray to you in time of need.
And in the flood of many waters they will draw near to
you.

[7] You are my refuge, and you will save me from trouble;
you will surround me with the joys of salvation.

[8] I will give you understanding and instruct you in the way
you will go; I will fix my eyes upon you.

[9] Do not become like horse and mule in which there is no
understanding; if you advance to restrain them by bit and
bridle they will not come near you.

[10] Many are the sorrows of the impious, but the one hoping
in the Lord will be surrounded with mercy.

[11] Be joyful in the Lord and rejoice, ye just; and exult, all
you upright in heart.

You should now be able to go through the psalm and identify
the nouns and the verbs. Underline the nouns, double underline
the verbs. Of course you will make some mistakes, but using what
you now know of the five declensions and the three conjugations
(out of four), you should be able to spot noun endings as opposed
to verb endings. You may want to draw a circle around adjectives.

Do that now, before I begin the analysis of the verses of the
psalm.

*   *   *   *   *   *

Okay. You've done your duty; now I'll do mine.

The Latin text set down above is that produced by the Pontifical Commission for a New Vulgate Edition of the Bible. It was set up by Paul VI, and the volume containing the Psalms was published in Vatican City in 1974. It differs not only from the Vulgate but also from the Psalter of Pius XII that necessitated new editions of the *Breviarium Romanum* when it appeared. When I was a boy in school, working after class in the library at Nazareth Hall, I would sometimes be set to work sorting through the books bequeathed the school by a priest alumnus who had died. Of course there would be breviaries, but they were the old ones that had been replaced. So I was allowed to take a set of them. Since Vatican II, the *Breviarium Romanum* has been replaced by most priests with an English *Liturgy of the Hours*. All the more reason for us to learn the psalm in the new vulgate version. (The Vulgate—that is, the putting of Scripture into the vernacular Latin undertaken by St. Jerome in the Fourth Century, settling in Bethlehem to do it; it was for centuries the benchmark and was the basis for the Douay-Rheims English translation. Medievalists find the Douay-Rheims preferable in supplying English versions of the Latin of medieval authors.)

1. **Beatus cui remissa est iniquitas.** The adjective **beatus** (nominative, singular, masculine) modifies the understood subject, the one, he. Who is the one blessed? The Pius XII version has **cujus** instead of **cui**, that is, a genitive instead of the dative in our version.

The Relative Pronoun

	Singular			Plural		
	Masc.	*Fem.*	*Neuter*	*Masc.*	*Fem.*	*Neut.*
Nom.	qui	quae	quod	qui	quae	quae
Gen.	cujus	cujus	cujus	quorum	quarum	quorum
Dat.	cui	cui	cui	quibus	quibus	quibus
Acc.	quem	quam	quod	quos	quas	quae
Abl.	quo	qua	quo	quibus	quibus	quibus

But whether *whose* (**cujus**) or *for whom* (**cui**), the one the psalmist calls blessed is the one whose sin or iniquity has been forgiven. **Iniquitas** is the subject of the passive past of **remitto**: *has been* *forgiven.* The participle, **remissa,** is the nominative singular feminine to agree with **iniquitas,** which is a feminine noun.

Blessed the one for whom sin has been forgiven; blessed the one whose sin has been forgiven. The dative **cui** could be called a "dative of possession," and then we would translate it as if it were the genitive.

* **et obtectum est peccatum.** The Pius XII Psalter gives it thus: **cujus obtectum est peccatum,** making it very clear that we have exactly the same construction as before. In our version, **cui** is understood, something conveyed by the conjunctive **et.** The one whose sin has been forgiven is blessed and whose sin has been covered over. The past passive here is **obtectum,** which with **est** forms the perfect passive, with **obtectum** in the nominative masculine singular of the participle in order to function as an adjective for **peccatum,** a neuter verb. **Obtectum** is interesting. The noun **tectum** means *roof* and, more generally, *covering.* It is derived from a verb in the third conjugation whose principal parts are **tego, tegere, texi, tectus.** The addition of the prepostion **ob** as its prefix gives us **obtego, obtegere, obtexi, obtectus** or in the neuter **obtectum.** Not just covered, but covered completely, buried.

2. **Beatus vir, cui non imputavit Dominus delictum.** Here the noun modified by **beatus** is explicit—**vir,** a man: *blessed the man, to whom the Lord does not impute guilt.* Here the dative of the relative pronoun, **cui**—agreeing in gender and number but not in case with the noun to which it relates—functions as a dative. To whom the Lord did not impute blame or guilt. **Imputat** is the present tense third person singular of **imputo** and the *Lord,* **Dominus,** is its subject. **Delictum,** the object of the verb is in the accusative case.

* **non est in spiritu eius dolus. Dolus** is a second declension noun (actually a loan word from Greek) and can be translated as *deceit* or *guilt.* The man who is blessed because his sins have been forgiven and his sin covered over is a man to whom the Lord imputes no guilt *nor is there deceit in his spirit.* That is, literally, *in the spirit of him.*

3. **Quoniam tacui, inveteraverunt ossa mea, dum rugirem tota die.**

Quoniam means since or *because;* the Pius XII Psalter has **quam-**

diu, *as long as;* **tacui**—this is the first person singular of the perfect tense of the second conjugation verb **tacere** whose principal parts are **taceo, tacere, tacui, tacitum.** So: *since or as long as I was silent,* **inveteraverunt ossa mea.** Those last two words are the subject of that long verb. **Os** is a neuter noun meaning *bone;* the nominative neuter plural is **ossa** with **mea** modifying it: *my bones.* And what are they doing? Well, the ending of that long verb tells you that it is third person plural and a perfect tense of **invetero, inveterare, inveteravi, inveteratus.** You can see that if we conjugated the perfect form, **inveteravi,** we would get **inveteraverunt.** And what did the bones of the psalmist do while he remained silent? They grew old.

   * **dum rugirem tota die. Dum** = *while;* **tota die,** both the noun and its adjective in the ablative = *the whole day long.* **Rugirem** = *I will groan.*

   4. Quoniam die ac nocte gravata est super me manus tua. The subject is at the end, **manus,** *hand,* modified by **tua,** since **manus** is a feminine noun. *Since or as long as your hand* **gravata est:** the passive perfect of the deponent verb—a deponent verb is one which has only passive forms—and means *has weighed* **super me** = *on me,* and then the adverbial phrase, **die ac nocte,** *day and night,* two ablatives having adverbial force.

   * **immutatus est vigor meus in ardoribus aestatis.** Since your hand was heavy upon me day and night, the psalmist says, **vigor meus** = *my strength,* the noun being masculine singular, so of course its adjective must be, **immutatus est** = *was changed,* **in ardoribus aestatis** = *under or in the heat(s) of summer.* **Ardoribus** is the ablative plural of **ardor** and **aestatis** the genitive of the noun for summer, aestas, aestatis, aestati, aestatem, aestate.

   5. Peccatum meum cognitum tibi feci. We begin at the end with the verb, which you recognize as the first person singular of the perfect tense of **facio** = *to do or to make. I made* **peccatum meum** = *my sin,* accusative case, **peccatum** being neuter, so its accusative and nominative are spelled the same, and **meum** modifies it. *I made my sin* **cognitum** = *known;* this is the participle of **cognoscor, cognosci, cognitus sum,** another deponent verb. So our verb is really **cognitum feci,** a compound = *I have made known, or I have made my sin known* **tibi,** *to you,* dative.

Personal Pronouns
First Person

	Singular	Plural
Nominative	ego, I	nos, we
Genitive	mei, mine	nostri, ours
Dative	mihi, to me	nobis, to us
Accusative	me, me	nos, us
Ablative	me, (from) me	nobis, (by) us

Second Person

	Singular	Plural
Nominative	tu, you	vos, you
Genitive	tui, of you	vestri, of you
Dative	tibi, to you	vobis, to you
Accusative	te, you	vos, you
Ablative	te, (by) you	vobis, (by) you

* et delictum meum non abscondi. Abscondi is the first person singular of the perfect tense of abscondo, abscondere, abscondi, absconditum, meaning hide or conceal. So: I did not conceal delictum meum, my guilt.

* Dixi: "Confitebor adversum me iniquitatem meam Domino."

Dixi = is the first person singular perfect of the third conjugation verb whose principal parts are dico, dicere, dixi, dictum, to say. So: I said. There follows a direct quote, which simplifies things in Latin. Confitebor is the first person singular of the future tense of the deponent verb Confiteri, confessus sum. Some of you will recognize its present tense: Confiteor, I confess, the prayer still heard in the Mass. So: I will confess adversum me, against myself. But what is the object of the verb? Iniquitatem meam. No problem there. Domino, to the Lord, a dative.

* Et tu remisisti impietatem peccati mei. Our tables giving personal pronouns come in handy here. And you remisisti = second person singular perfect tense of our old friend remittere, of which tu is the subject here. You forgave impietatem peccati mei = the impiety of my sin.

6. Propter hoc orabit ad te omnis sanctus in tempore oppor-

tuno. The sentence begins with **propter hoc,** the preposition, *on account of, because of,* governs the accusative, hence **hoc** = *this.* *Because of this,* **omnis sanctus** = *every holy one,* nominative case and the subject of the verb **orabit** = *will pray,* **ad te** = *to you,* and when? **tempore opportuno** = *at an opportune or fitting time,* the noun and its adjective both in the ablative.

Let's have before us tables of demonstrative pronouns, **hic, haec, hoc,** *this;* **is, ea, id,** *he, she, it;* **ille, illa, illud,** *that.*

Demonstrative Pronouns

	Singular				*Plural*		
	Masc.	*Fem.*	*Neut.*		*Masc.*	*Fem.*	*Neut.*
Nom.	hic	haec	hoc		hi	hae	haec
Gen.	huius	huius	huius		horum	harum	horum
Dat.	huic	huic	huic		his	his	his
Acc.	hunc	hanc	hoc		hos	has	haec
Abl.	hoc	hac	hoc		his	his	his
Nom.	is	ea	id		ei	eae	ea
Gen.	eius	eius	eius		eorum	earum	eorum
Dat.	ei	ei	ei		eis	eis	eis
Acc.	eum	eam	id		eos	eas	ea
Abl.	eo	ea	eo		eis	eis	eis
Nom.	ille	illa	illud		illi	illae	illa
Gen.	illius	illius	illius		illarum	illorum	illorum
Dat.	illi	illi	illi		illis	illis	illis
Acc.	illum	illam	illud		illos	illas	illa
Abl.	illo	illa	illo		illis	illis	illis

* **Et in diluvio aquarum multarum ad eum non approximabunt.**

And in a flood: **diluvio** is the ablative of the neuter noun **diluvium.** *Of many waters:* **multarum aquarum.** The genitive plural of **aqua** is modified by the genitive plural of **multa.** The verb **approximabunt** is in the future tense = *they will not draw near* **ad eum,** *to him.* The subject of the verb is those many waters, understood, and thus in the nominative case.

But let us consider the future tense.

Future Active Tense
First Conjugation

Singular	*Plural*
1. amabo	amabimus
2. amabis	amabitis
3. amabit	amabunt

Second Conjugation

1. monebo	monebimus
2. monebis	monebitis
3. monebit	monebunt

Third Conjugation

1. regam	regemus
2. reges	regetis
3. reget	regent

7. **Tu es refugium meum, a tribulatione conservabis me;** *Thou, you, my refuge,* **conservabis,** *you will preserve me.* **Conservabis** is the second person singular of the future tense of **conservo, conservare, conservavi, conservatus,** a verb of the first conjugation. Preserve from what? **A tribulatione,** *from tribulation.*

* **exsultationibus salutis circumdabis me. Circumdabis** is another second person singular of the future tense of a first conjugation verb, formed of **circum** and **do, dare, dedi, datus,** *to give.* The compound verb means to surround. So: *you will surround me;* **exsultationibus,** an ablative plural, *with the delights,* **salutis,** the genitive singular of **salus, salutis, saluti, salutem, salute.** *You will surround me with the delights of salvation.*

8. **Intellectum tibi dabo et instruam te in via, qua gradieris;** **dabo,** I will give; **intellectum,** the accusative of this fourth declension noun:

Fourth Declension

	Singular	*Plural*
Nom.	intellectus	intellectus
Gen.	intellectus	intellectuum
Dat.	intellectui	intellectibus
Acc.	intellectum	intellectus
Abl.	intellectu	intellectibus

* **firmabo super te oculos meos.** Another future tense, first person singular, of a first conjugation verb, **firmo, firmare, firmavi, firmatus.** *I will fix* **oculos meos,** accusative plural, *my eyes,* **super te,** *on you.*

9. **Nolite fieri sicut equus et mulus. Nolite,** this is an imperative of the irregular verb **nolo, nolle nolui,** which is always linked with two others, **volo, velle, volui,** and **malo, malle, malui. Velle,** to wish or be willing; **nolle,** *to be unwilling;* **malle,** *to wish rather or prefer.* Here are the three in the present tense.

	Singular			*Plural*	
1. volo	nolo	malo	volumus	nolumus	malumus
2. vis	non vis	mavis	vultis	non vultus	malvultus
3. vult	non vult	mavult	volunt	nolunt	malunt

So: *do not be willing* **fieri.** This is the infinitive of the irregular verb **fio, fieri, factus sum.** *Be unwilling to become* **sicut equus et mulus,** *like horse and mule.*

* **quibus non est intellectus in camo et freno;** the dative plural of the relative pronoun refers to the horse and mule *in which* **non est intellectus,** *there is not understanding,* **in camo et freno,** *in bit and bridle.* Perhaps: *in which there is no understanding in bit and bridle.*

* **si accedis ad constringendum, non approximant te. Accedis,** second person singular of the third conjugation verb **accedo, accedere, accessi, accessum.** *If you approach* **ad constringendum** *to restrain (them),* **non approximant te,** *they will not come near you.*

You will wonder about **constringendum.** It is a verb, a form of **constringo, constringere, constrinxi, constrinctum,** but what form is it? This form, **amandum, petendum, constringendum,** is called the gerundive, a verbal noun like the English *loving, seeking, restraining,* which is always introduced by a preposition, as here by **ad,** *for.*

The gerundive should not be confused with the gerund, a verbal adjective which is formed in the same way as the gerundive but which, as an adjective, has masculine and feminine as well as neuter forms—e.g. **amandus, amanda, amandum; monendus, monenda, monendum; capiendus, capienda, capiendum; audiendus, audienda, audiendum; utendus, utenda, utendum.** These have a passive sense: *to be loved; to be advised; to be taken; to be heard; to be used.* **Illa amanda est,** *she ought to be loved;* **ille monendus est,** *he ought to be advised.*

10. **Multi dolores impii:** many are the sorrows of the impious. The verb to be is understood.

* **sperantem autem in Domino misericordia circumdabit.**

What is the subject? **Misericordia,** *mercy,* **circumdabit,** *will surround,* **sperantem,** *one hoping*—this is the accusative of the present participle of **spero, sperare, speravi, speratus.** One hoping in **Domino** *in the Lord.* **Autem** means *but* or *however.* Thus this verse of the psalm reads: *Many are the sorrows of the impious, but mercy will surround one hoping in the Lord.*

11. **Laetamini in Domino et exsultate, iusti, et gloriamini, omnes recti corde.** **Laetamini** is the plural imperative in the passive form, but of a deponent verb—that is a verb which exists only in the passive form which however has an active meaning. So: *Rejoice,* in the sense of, you or ye rejoice, and **exsultate,** another plural imperative, *rejoice,* **in Domino,** *in the Lord.* Who is being addressed? **iusti,** *the just,* or *ye just.* So: *rejoice in the Lord and exult, ye just.* And it continues, with another deponent verb's plural imperative, **gloriamini,** *glory,* or *glory in,* referring back to the Lord, not the just this time, but **omnes** *all,* a nominative masculine plural, modified by **recti,** *right,* **corde,** ablative singular. *Rejoice and exult in the Lord, ye just, and glory (in the Lord) all rectified in heart.*

Psalm 129, De Profundis

1. De profundis clamo ad te, Domine,
   Domine, audi vocem meam.
2. Fiant aures tuae intentae
   ad vocem obsecrationis meae.
3. Si delictorum memoriam servaveris, Domine,
   Domine, quis sustinebit?
4. Sed penes te est peccatorum venia,
   ut cum reverentia serviatur tibi.
5. Spero in Dominum
   sperat anima mea in verbum ejus;
6. Exspectat anima mea Dominum
   magis quam custodes auroram.
7. Magis quam custodes auroram,
   exspectet Israel Dominum.
8. Quia penes Dominum misericordia
   et copiosa penes eum redemptio:
9. Et ipse redimet Israel
   ex omnibus iniquitatibus ejus.

1. **De profundis clamo ad te, Domine, Domine, audi vocem mean.**

De profundis: out of the depths. The noun is **profundum,** and we have here the ablative plural, governed by the preposition **de.** It is the psalmist who speaks: first person singular present tense of **clamare,** a first conjugation verb. *I cry out* **ad te, Domine:** *to thee, Lord.* **Te** is the accusative after the preposition **ad, Domine** is in the vocative. *Out of the depths, I cry to thee, O Lord.*

Lord is repeated, and then the deprecatory imperative of **audire,** to hear, heed, listen, taking the accusative of **vox, vocis,** namely **vocem,** which is modified by the singular feminine accusative **meam,** which tells you the gender of **vox.** *Lord, hear my voice . . .*

2. **Fiant aures tuae intentae ad vocem obsecrationis meae.**

Fiant is the third person plural subjunctive of **fio, fieri, factus sum,** the passive forms of **facere.** The phrase **fiat lux** will be familiar: *let there be light, let light come to be.* **Aures tuae** = *your ears,* nominative plural. *Let your ears become* **intentae.** This is the past participle of **intendere,** and it is nominative plural feminine in order to agree in gender number and case with **aures.** *Let your ears become attentive.* To what? **Ad vocem**—*to the voice.* What voice? **Obsecrationis meae** = *of my prayer. Let your ears be attentive to the voice of my supplication.*

3. **Si delictorum memoriam servaveris, Domine, Domine, quis sustinebit?**

Si, *if,* will introduce the subjunctive: *if it were* as opposed to *it is.* What verb does it govern? **Servaveris** is a first conjugation verb and, paradigmatically—that is, with an eye to the grammatical appendix in the back of the book—we will think of **amaveris,** which is the second person singular of the perfect subjunctive. If you should have preserved **memoriam delictorum:** *the memory of wicked deeds, Lord, Lord,* **quis sustinebit** = *who will bear it,* a future third person singular whose subject is the pronoun **quis.** *Lord, if you were mindful of sins, who could survive, Lord?*

4. **Sed penes te est peccatorum venia, ut cum reverentia serviatur tibi.**

The preposition **penes** occurs three times in this psalm: it is all but synonymous with **cum. Venia,** feminine noun, meaning *grace, favor, pardon. But with you is pardon of sins.* Why? **Ut** here means *in order that* and introduces the subjunctive **serviatur,** from **servire.** *In order that it might be served to you, or with respect to you* = *in order that you might be served.* How? **Cum reverentia.** *With reverence.*

5. **Spero in Dominum, sperat anima mea in verbum ejus;**

Spero is a standard first conjugation verb, meaning *to hope:* we have it in the first person singular present tense, and also in the third person, **sperat.** *I hope in the Lord, my soul hopes in his word.* Literally, *on the word of him.*

6. **Exspectat anima mea Dominum magis quam custodes auroram.**

Anima is the subject of the verb **exspectat** and is modified by **mea** and has for its object **Dominum:** *My soul looks to the Lord.* How much? **Magis** means *more* or *rather,* and **quam** here means *than—more than the sentry (looks for or awaits) the dawn.*

7. Magis quam custodes auroram, exspectet Israel Dominum.
The effective comparison is repeated: *more than the sentry looks for the dawn, Israel looks for or awaits the Lord.* The Latin is pellucid.

8. Quia penes Dominum misericordia et copiosa penes eum redemptio.
Why? **Quia,** *because,* **penes Dominum,** *with the Lord,* **misericordia.** The verb to be is understood: *Because with the Lord there is mercy.* **Copiosa** modifies **redemptio,** the nominative of the feminine verb meaning *the buying back or redemption:* the adjective means what you think it means: *copious, abundant.* **penes eum:** *with him,* that is, *with the Lord. And with him is abundant redemption.*

9. Et ipse redimet Israel ex omnibus iniquitatibus ejus.
Ipse, *he,* that is, *the Lord, will redeem Israel.* **Redimet** is future. Explain why. Redeem from what? **Ex omnibus iniquitatibus ejus.** *From all its iniquities.* The genitive **ejus** refers of course to Israel.

Psalm 109, Dixit Dominus

THIS WAS THE FIRST OF THE FIVE PSALMS recited—or more often, it being a Sunday, sung—at Sunday Vespers according to the *Breviarium Romanum*.

1. **Dixit Dominus Domino meo: "Sede a dextris meis,**
   donec ponam inimicos tuos scabellum pedum tuorum."
2. **Sceptrum potentiae tuae protendet Dominus ex Sion:**
   "Dominare in medio inimicorum tuorum!
3. **Tecum principatus die ortus tui in splendore sanctitatis:**
   ante luciferum, tamquam rorem, genui te."
4. **Juravit Dominus et non poenitebit eum:**
   "Tu es sacerdos in aeternum secundum ordinem
   Melchisedech."
5. **Dominus a dextris tuis:**
   conteret die irae suae reges.
6. **Judicabit nationes, acervabit cadavera;**
   conteret capita late per terram.
7. **De torrente in via bibet,**
   propterea extollet caput.

1. **Dixit Dominus Domino meo: "Sede a dextris meis,**
   Dixit, the third person singular of the perfect active of third conjugation verb **dicere,** *to say;* its subject is **Dominus** and its indirect object is **Domino:** *the Lord said to my lord.* What? **Sede,** the imperative of the second conjugation verb **sedere,** *to sit;* where? **a dextris meis,** *at my right hand.* For how long?

   * **donec ponam inimicos tuos scabellum pedum tuorum."**
   Donec, *until,* **ponam,** the subjunctive of **ponere,** a third conjugation verb: *until I might put,* **inimicos tuos,** *your enemies,* **scabellum,** this would be the accusative, so as to be in apposition to the direct object of **ponam:** *as a footstool,* **pedum tuorum.** That is the

genitive plural of **pes, pedis,** a third declension noun. *Until I might put your enemies as the footstool of your feet.*

2. Sceptrum potentiae tuae protendet Dominus ex Sion:

Protendet, this is the future of the third conjugation verb **pro-tendere,** to stretch forth, to stretch out; its subject is **Dominus;** its direct object is the accusative **sceptrum,** a neuter of the second declension: **potentiae tuae,** *of your power,* **ex Sion:** *the Lord will extend the scepter of your power out of Sion.* Why?

* "Dominare in medio inimicorum tuorum!

The Lord speaks. **Dominare** is the imperative of the first conjugation verb **dominari:** *that you might rule or dominate.* Where? In **medio inimicorum tuorum:** *in the midst of your enemies.*

3. Tecum principatus die ortus tui in splendore sanctitatis:

Tecum = cum te, principatus, -us, m., a fourth declension noun = *the first place, preeminence,* **die ortus tui:** that is the ablative of **dies, diei,** *on the day of your birth:* **ortus, -us,** m., is fourth declension. *Preeminence is with you on or from the day of your rising or birth,* in **splendore sanctitatis:** *in the splendor of holiness.*

* ante luciferum, tamquam rorem, genui te."

Ante luciferum: *before the morning star,* **tamquam rorem:** the adverb **tamquam** means *as, just as, like.* Like what? **Rorem** is the accusative of **ros, roris,** m., meaning *dew.* **Genui** is the first person singular perfect of **gigno, gignere, genui, genitum,** *to beget, to give birth, I gave birth to you,* **te.** *With you is preeminence from the day of your birth in the splendor of holiness; like dew before the dawn I have begotten you.*

4. Juravit Dominus et non poenitebit eum:

Juravit, perfect from **jurare,** first conjugation, *to swear.* Its subject is **Dominus:** *the Lord swore,* **et non poenitebit eum:** from the second conjugation verb **poenitere:** it occurs here in the future active. *The Lord has sworn and he will not regret it.*

* "Tu es sacerdos in aeternum secundum ordinem Melchisedech."

Sacerdos, sacerdotis, m., *priest. Thou art a priest* in **aeternum:** *unto eternity, forever;* **secundum ordinem Melchisedech:** *according to the order of Melchsiedech.*

5. **Dominus a dextris tuis: conteret die irae suae reges.**

Dominus a dextris tuis: the verb is understood: *the Lord is at your right hand.* **Conterere,** third conjugation, *to crush, grind, rub out.* Used here in the third person singular of the future tense: its subject is **Dominus. Reges** is accusative plural of **rex, regis. Die,** ablative expressing time when: **irae,** genitive of the first declension noun **ira, irae,** *wrath. He will crush kings on the day of his wrath.*

6. **Judicabit nationes, acervabit cadavera; conteret capita late per terram.**

Judicabit, future active of **judicare,** whose direct object is **nationes,** nominative plural of **natio, nationis; acervabit,** another future active, this one from **acervare,** *to heap or pile,* whose direct object is **cadavera,** accusative plural of **cadaver, cadaveris,** n. So: *He will judge nations, he will heap up corpses.* **Conteret,** another future, whose object is **capita,** accusative plural of **caput, capitis,** *head.* **Late** is an adverb from the adjective **latus, lata, latum,** and means *widely.* Where? **Per terram** = *throughout the land. He will crack heads widely throughout the land or even, throughout the breadth of the land.*

7. **De torrente in via bibet, propterea extollet caput.**

Bibet, a third person singular of the future active of **bibo, bibere, bibi, bibitus,** to drink. He will drink what? **De torrente,** *from the torrent,* **in via,** *along the way;* **extollet,** another future; *he will lift up.* What? **Caput. Propterea,** adverb, *on that account, wherefore. He will drink from the torrent along the way; wherefore he will lift up his head.*

Lesson Ten
Readings from the New Testament

YOU ARE ABOUT TO DISCOVER that you can easily make out the Gospels in Latin. Not simply because the passages we will be studying are already familiar to you but also because the Latin you have already learned puts the following ten passages within your reach. Guidance to translating will be given in footnotes.

1. Matthew 16:24–28

24. Tunc[1] Iesus dixit discipulis suis:[2] "Si quis[3] vult post me venire, abneget[4] semetipsum et tollat crucem suam et sequatur me.

25. Qui enim voluerit[5] animam suam salvam facere, perdet eam; qui autem perdiderit animam suam propter me, inveniet eam.[6]

1   Adverb, then, at that point in time.
2   Dative plural of **discipulus, -i** as indirect object of the third person perfect active of **dicere** (3): *Then Jesus said to his disciples.*
3   Relative pronoun; here = *anyone. If anyone wishes to come after me. . . .*
4   This is a subjunctive called for by the initial mark of a hypothetical, **si; abnegare** (1), so this is third person present active subjunctive whose subject is **quis**. Its direct object is the reflexive pronoun **semetipsum** = *himself*. **Tollat** is the same subjunctive from **tollo, tollere, sustuli, sublatum** (3) and **sequatur** the same of the deponent **sequor, sequi, secutus sum** (3). **Vult** is 3rd person singular present of **velle**: *to will. Let him deny himself and take up his cross and follow me.*
5   **Voluerit** is the perfect active subjunctive of **velle** = *would wish*; its subject is **qui; enim** means *for: for he who would* **facere**, *would make,* **salvam**, *safe,* in the accusative feminine singular first declension, to agree with the object of **facere**, namely, **animam**. **Perdet** is the third person singular future active, of **perdere** (3); **eam**, agrees with **animam**. *For he who would save his soul will lose it.*
6   Here the thought is reversed: **perdiderit** is in the perfect active subjunctive and **inveniet**—from **invenire** (4)—is in the future indicative. **Autem** = *however, but.* **Propter me** = *on account of me.*

26. Quid enim prodest[7] homini, si mundum universum lucretur, animae vero suae detrimentum patiatur? Aut[8] quam dabit homo commutationem pro anima sua?

27. Filius enim hominis venturus est[9] in gloria Patris sui cum angelis suis, et tunc reddet unicuique secundum opus eius.

28. Amen dico vobis: Sunt quidam[10] de hic stantibus, qui non gustabunt mortem, donec videant Filium hominis venientem in regno suo."

Anima is perhaps best translated as *life;* to lose one's soul for Christ makes no sense outside of a Graham Greene novel, whereas to give up control over one's life to him does.

7   **Prodest** is from **prosum, profui, prodesse,** *to be advantageous to.* **Quid,** interrogative: *what?* Here we might render it *How. What does it promote or advance for a man* ... **Si:** *if,* and we look for a subjunctive and find it: **lucretur,** a deponent (**lucror** = *to gain*) of the first conjugation, so this is the passive form of present subjunctive. Its object is **mundum,** modified by **universum** = *whole world. If he should gain the whole world* ... **Vero,** adverb, *in truth, indeed, truly, in fact.* **Patiatur,** from the third conjugation deponent **patior,** so this is the third person singular subjunctive. **Animae suae** = dative. *But a detriment with respect to his soul should be suffered.*

8   **Aut,** this disjunctive is stronger than **vel** and carries the note of the one thing and not the other. **Quam,** relative, accusative singular, agreeing with **commutationem; dabit,** a simple future active from **dare** (1). *Or what exchange will a man give for his own soul.*

9   **Venturus est,** future perfect from **venire; Filius hominis,** *the Son of Man,* Christ's usual way of referring to himself: *he will come in the glory.* **Patris sui,** *of his Father,* **cum angelis suis,** *with his angels,* **et tunc,** *and then* **reddet,** a future from **reddere** (3) *will render.* **Unicuique,** a dative from **unusquisque,** *to each, each one.* **Secundum,** *according to, following on,* **opus eius,** *the work of him, his work.*

10   **Quidam,** the subject of **sunt:** *there are some,* **de stantibus,** the ablative plural of the present participle of **sto, stare, steti, status,** *to stand: among those standing* **hic,** an adverb, *here* [**hic et nunc** = *here and now*]. **Gustabunt,** third person plural future of **gustare** (1), *to taste, to know,* **mortem,** accusative singular of **mors, mortis,** f. **Donec,** *until,* **videant,** from **videre** (2) so this is subjunctive: *until they see.* **Venientem** is the present participle of **venire,** in the accusative to agree with **Filium:** *the Son of man coming* in **regno suo,** *in his royalty. Amen, I say to you: There are some standing here who will not taste death until they will see the Son of Man coming in his royalty.*

2. Matthew 7:7–11

7. Petite, et dabitur vobis;[1] quaerite et invenietis; pulsate, et aperietur vobis.

8. Omnis enim qui petit, accipit; et qui quaerit, invenit; et pulsanti aperietur.[2]

9. Aut quis ex vobis homo,[3] quem si petierit filius suus panem, numquid lapidem porriget ei?

10. Aut si piscem petierit, numquid serpentem porriget ei?[4]

---

1   Petite, plural imperative of peto, petire, petivi, petitus, to seek or ask; dabitur, third person plural passive of dare, to give. Vobis, dative plural of the personal pronoun. Ask and it will be given to you. Quaerite, ditto of Quaerere (3), to seek; invenietis, second person plural future active of invenire (4); pulsate, the plural imperative of pulsare (1), to knock, aperietur: future passive third person singular of aperire (4), to open, so here: it will be opened vobis, to you.

2   Omnis, everyone, all, is our subject, qui, a relative pronoun, who; then, qui petit . . . qui quaerit: two third person singulars of the present active of their respective verbs; accipere (3) and invenire (3) accipit . . . invenit. Present tenses too. And then a shift: pulsanti is the dative singular of the present participle of pulsare and aperietur is a future passive: to the one knocking it will be opened. Everyone who asks, receives, and who seeks, finds; and to the one knocking it will be opened.

3   Quis homo, what man, ex vobis, from among you,quem whom, the accusative, the object of petierit, from our friend petire, a third person singular subjective perfect, object = panem, accusative of panis, panis, m. (3). Numquid, never, porriget from porrigo, porrigere, porrexi, porrectus (3), to reach out, extend: the form is third person singular future indicative active, ei, dative, the indirect object of will extend, whose direct object is lapidem, from lapis, lapidis, m., a stone. Or what man among you, if his son asks for bread, will ever hand him a stone?

4   The same construction, with piscem, from piscis, piscis, m, fish, the object of petierit, and serpentem, from serpens, serpentis, snake, as object of porriget.

11. Si ergo vos, cum sitis mali,[5] nostis dona bona dare filiis vestris, quanto magis Pater vester, qui in caelis est, dabit bona petentibus se.[6]

---

5   **Sitis** is the second person plural of the present subjunctive of **esse**, following on **cum**, meaning *when or since:* **mali**, nominative plural to agree with **vos**. **Nostis** is a second person plural present indicative active of **nosco, noscere, novi, notus** (3): know what? **Dare,** *to give* what, **dona bona,** *good gifts,* **donum, -i,** n. To whom? **Filiis vestris,** *to your children.*

6   **Quanto** = *how much,* **magis,** *more, so:* how much more, **dabit,** *will give.* Who? **Pater vester,** *your Father,* **qui in caelis est,** an echo of the Lord's Prayer. Will give what? **Bona,** *good things,* an accusative neuter plural. To whom? **Petentibus,** *to those asking,* dative plural of the present participle of **peto; se** is the reflexive object of the participle.

3. Matthew 5:43–48

43. Audistis quia dictum est:[1] "Diliges proximum tuum et odio habebis inimicum tuum."[2]

44. Ego autem dico vobis:[3] Diligite inimicos vestros et orate pro persequentibus vos,

45. ut sitis filii Patris vestri,[4] qui in caelis est, quia solem suum oriri facit super malos et bonos et pluit super iustos et iniustos.

46. Si enim dilexeritis[5] eos, qui vos diligunt, quam mercedem habetis? Nonne et publicani hoc faciunt?[6]

---

1   **Audistis,** second person, perfect active of **audire** (3), a variant on **audivistis,** *you have heard.* **Quia,** *that:* not a construction we would expect in classical Latin. **Dictum est:** perfect passive: *it has been said. You have heard that it was said:*

2   The verbs here are future indicative actives, **diliges,** from **diligere** (3), **habebis** from **habere** (2), **you will love, you will have or hold,** the object of the first, **proximum,** *the one next, neighbor,* **tuum,** *your;* **odio,** *to hold or have in hate* = *you will hate,* **inimicum,** *enemy,* **tuum,** *your. You will love your neighbor and hate your enemy.*

3   **Autem,** *however,* a switch of thought: **ego autem dico vobis:** *But I tell you.* And now the plural imperative of **diligere: diligite,** and of **orare: orate.** Love whom? **Inimicos vestros.** Pray for whom? **Pro persequentibus:** ablative plural of the present participle of **persequor,** *for those pursuing or persecuting* **vos,** *you. Love your enemies and pray for those who persecute you.*

4   Why? **ut sitis,** *in order that you might be,* a subjunctive of **esse** following **ut;** be what? **Filii Patris vestri,** *children of your Father,* and then another echo of the **Pater noster.** Why will obeying verse 44 make us to be sons of the Father? **Quia,** *because,* **facit oriri solem suum:** *he makes his sun to rise,* **super malos et bonos,** *on the bad and the good;* and **pluit,** from **pluo, plere, plui, pletus,** *rain.* Where does it rain? **Super iustos et iniustos,** *on the just and the unjust,* the substantives formed from the adjectives **iustus, -a, -um,** and **iniustus, a-, -um.** As objects of the verb they are accusative plural.

47. Et si salutaveritis fratres vestros tantum,[7] quid amplius facitis? Nonne et ethnici hoc faciunt?

48. Estote ergo vos perfecti, sicut Pater vester caelestis perfectus est.[8]

---

5   **Dilexeritis,** is the second person plural perfect subjunctive of **diligere** (3): *for if you should love,* **eos,** accusative plural, *those,* **qui vos diligunt,** *who love you,* the verb is present active indicative third person plural. **Quam mercedem:** the interrogative *what* modifies the accusative singular of the feminine noun **merces, mercedis,** *reward, pay.* **Habebitis:** second person plural future active, *will you have? For if you should love those who love you, what reward will you have?*

6   **Nonne** introduces a question expecting an affirmative answer. **Faciunt** has **publicani** for its subject. *Do not the publicans too* (**et**) *do* **hoc,** *this?*

7   **Salutaveritis,** like **dilexeritis** in verse 46, although a first conjugation verb, **salutare. Tantum** = *only. If you should greet only your brothers,* **quid amplius,** *what more,* **facitis,** *do you do?* **Ethnici,** a word revived recently: it means here *gentiles, peoples other than Jews.*

8   **Estote,** plural imperative of **esse; ergo,** *therefore,* drawing out the implications of what has been said; **vos,** subject of the imperative; **perfecti,** what you are to be. Perfect like whom? **Sicut Pater vester caelestis:** *your heavenly Father. Be ye perfect then as your heavenly Father is perfect.*

4. Mark 10:23–27

23. Et cirumspiciens Iesus ait discipulis suis:[1] "Quam difficile est, qui pecunias habent, in regnum Dei introibunt."[2]

24. Discipuli autem obstupescebant[3] in verbis eius. At Jesus rursus respondens ait illis:[4] "Filii, quam difficile est in regnum Dei introire,

25. Facilius est camelum per foramen acus transire quam divitem intrare in regnum Dei."[5]

---

1   Circumspiciens, an adjective formed from the present participle of circumspicere (3) modifies Iesus the subject of ait, from aio, a defective verb, *to say yes, affirm,* discipulis suis, indirect object, dative plural. *And, looking about, Jesus said to his disciples.*

2   Quam difficile, *how difficult;* qui relates to both habent and introibunt, the first present, the second future. Pecunias, from pecunia, -ae; in *into,* taking the accusative regnum. *How hard it is for those who have money, that they will enter . . .*

3   From obstupesco, obstupescere, obstupui, obstuptus,(3) *to become stupid, to be astounded:* third person plural imperfect active. In verbis eius: literally *in,* better here, *at his words. The disciples however were astounded at his words.*

4   At, conjunction, but, moreover; rursus, adverb, *back, on the contrary, on the other hand;* respondens, present participle of respondere (2) modifying Jesus, illis, dative, *to them.* In the repetition of the thought quam difficile takes the infinitive introire: *how hard it is to enter . . . But Jesus on the contrary replying said to them: "Sons, how difficult it is to enter the Kingdom of God.*

5   Facilius is the comparative of facilis, *easy,* thus, *easier.* Indirect discourse: camelum is the subject of the infinitive transire, *it is easier for a camel to pass through* foramen, -is, n. So this is an accusative following per; acus, acus, f., *needle.* Quam correlative of facilius, *easier than;* divitem, from dives, divitis, *rich,* intrare: accusative + infinitive as with camelum and pertransire. *It is easier for a camel to pass through the eye of a needle than for a rich man to enter the Kingdom of God."*

26. Qui magis admirabantur dicentes ad semetipsos:[6] "Et quis potest salvus fieri?"[7]

27. Intuens illos Iesus ait:[8] "Apud homines impossibile est sed non apud Deum: omnia enim possibilia sunt apud Deum."[9]

---

6   **Admirabantur** is from the deponent **admiror** (1) and is the imperfect indicative active; modified by the the adverb **magis; ad semetipsos:** *to themselves;* **dicentes** modifying the disciples referred back to by **qui,** *who. Who wondered the more, saying among themselves.*

7   **Fieri,** passive infinitive of **facere** following **potest,** from the compound verb **possum, posse, potui (potis + sum),** **potest,** third person singular present indicative active: *can be. Who can be saved?*

8   **Intuens,** from **intueor,** modifying Jesus the subject of **ait:** literally, *looking within them, Jesus said.*

9   **Apud homines . . . apud Deum:** *with or for men, with or for God:* **impossibile est:** *it is impossible.* **Possibilia** the predicate noun before **sunt** and matching the subject **omnia.** *All things are possible with God.*

5. Mark 12:13–17

13. **Et mittunt ad eum quosdam ex pharisaeis et herodianis**[1]**, ut eum caperent in verbo.**

14. **Qui venientes dicunt ei:**[2] **"Magister, scimus quia verax es et non curas quemquam,**[3] **nec enim vides in faciem hominum, sed in veritate viam Dei doces.**[4] **Licet dare tributum Caesari an non? Dabimus an non dabimus?"**[5]

15. **Qui sciens versutiam eorum ait illis:**[6] **"Quid me tentatis? Afferte mihi denarium, ut videam."**[7]

---

1   **Mittunt,** third person plural from **mittere** (3) whose object is **quosdam,** accusative plural masculine, *some,* **ad eum,** *to him, some,* **ex pharasaeis et herodianis,** *from those associated with the Pharisees and Herod.* Why? **Ut caperent eum,** that is the third person plural subjunctive of **capere** (3), *to take, that they might catch him,* in **verbo,** *in word, in what he said.*

2   The present participle, nominative plural, of **venire** (3), **venientes** goes with **qui,** *who, coming or arriving,* **dicunt ei,** *say to him.*

3   **Magister, magistri,** m. Here the vocative. *Teacher, master.* **Scimus quia,** *we know that:* the verb is present indicative active of **scio** (3): **verax es,** *you are truthful*—**verax, veracis.** **Non curas quemquam:** *you do not take care of anyone: worry about anyone.*

4   **Facies, faciei,** f., *external form or figure,* also *manner, kind:* **nec,** *nor do you look,* **vides, in faciem hominum,** literally, *in the face of men, to what men think,* **sed,** *but,* **doces,** *you teach,* from **docere** (2). **viam Dei,** *the way or path of God,* **in veritate,** *in truth:* **veritas, veritatis,** f.

5   **Licet, licuit, licitum est,** *it is allowed, one can or may,* **dare tributum,** *to give tribute,* **Caesari,** dative, **an non,** *or not?* **Dabimus,** first person plural, *we will give. Will we give or will we not give?*

6   **Versutia, -ae,** f., *cunning, craftiness.* **Qui** is a relative pronoun relating to the subject of **ait,** *he says or replies* (and modified by **sciens** whose object is **versutiam**): *who knowing their craftiness says,* **illis,** *to them.*

7   **Quid,** *what, for what, why:* **tentatis,** second person plural present active of **tentare** (1) *test, try, tempt.* **Afferte**—plural imperative, from **ad-ferre,** *to bring to, to bear toward;* **mihi,** dative, *to me,* **denarium,** *a denarium,* a unit of money, **ut videam,** *in order that,* followed by

16. At illi attulerunt.[8] Et ait illis: "Cuius est imago haec et inscriptio?"[9] Illi autem dixerunt ei: "Caesaris."[10]

17. Iesus autem dixit illis: "Quae sunt Caesaris, reddite Caesari et, quae sunt Dei, Deo." Et mirabantur super eo.[11]

---

subjunctive present active, first person singular, **videre** (2).

8   **Attulerunt** is the third person plural perfect active of **adferre: adfero, adferre, attuli, allatum** (or **adlatum**).

9   **Cujus**, genitive singular, *of whom;* **imago haec**, *this image,* **et inscriptio**, *and inscription:* **imago, imaginis; inscriptio, inscriptionis.** *Whose image and inscription is this (are these)?*

10   **Caesaris.** Genitive singular: objective genitive following on image and inscription, understood.

11   **Reddite,** plural imperative of **reddere** (3), its object is **quae sunt Caesaris,** *what are of Caesar, those things that are Caesar's.* **Deo,** indirect object of the understood **reddite. Mirabantur,** third person plural imperfect active of deponent **miror** (1). **Super** takes the ablative here: *about him.*

6. Luke 9:18–22

18. Et factum est cum solus esset orans,[1] erant cum illo discipuli, et interrogavit illos dicens: "Quem me dicunt esse turbae?"[2]

19. At illi responderunt et dixerunt:[3] "Ioannem Baptistam, alii autem Eliam, alii vero: Propheta unus de prioribus surrexit."

20. Dixit autem illis: "Vos autem quem me esse dicitis?" Respondens Petrus dixit: "Christum Dei."

21. At ille increpans[4] illos praecepit, ne cui dicerent hoc,

---

1   **Factum est,** *it happened, it came about,* **cum,** *when,* taking the subjunctive **esset,** *he was,* **solus,** *alone,* **orans,** present participle of **orare** (1), *praying;* **erant,** third person plural imperfect indicative active, *were;* its subject? **discipuli,** *the disciples were* **cum illo,** *with him;* **et interrogavit eos:** a third person singular perfect indicative active of **interrogare** (1). **Dicens,** present participle of **dicere** (3), *saying. And it came about that when he was praying alone and his disciples were with him, he interrogated them, saying:*

2   **Turba, -ae,** f., *tumult, uproar;* **turbae,** *crowds,* the subject of **dicunt,** whose object is **quem,** *whom do the crowds say* **me esse,** indirect discourse (accusative + infinitive) after **dicere:** *whom do the crowds say I am?*

3   Two third person plural perfect actives, one of **respondere,** the other of **dicere. Ioannem Baptistam,** accusative as object of implied 'say'; **alii vero,** nominative plural masculine, **alius, alia, aliud; Eliam** in accusative. Now a grammatical shift after the repeated **alii vero,** direct as opposed to indirect speech: *one prophet,* **de prioribus,** *from the earlier ones, from earlier times,* **surrexit,** third person singular perfect indicative active from **surgere** (3).

4   Verse 20 will give you no problems. **Increpans,** present participle, modifying Jesus, from **increpare,** *to make a noise,* **praecepit,** from **praecipere** (4), a perfect indicative active. **Ne,** *lest,* **dicerent,** subjunctive after **ne,** *they should say,* **hoc,** *this,* **cui,** *to anyone.*

22. dicens: "Oportet Filium hominis multa pati et reprobari a
    senioribus et principibus sacerdotum et scribis et occidi et
    tertia die resurgere."[5]

---

5   **Oportet,** *it is fitting, it is necessary:* this will be followed by a phrase
whose subject will be accusative and its verb infinitive: **Filium . . .
pati et reprobari . . . occidi . . . resurgere. Multa** is the object of *suffer,*
pati (from the deponent **Patior, pati, passus sum**); *to be rejected,* **a
senioribus et principibus sacerdotum et scribis:** *by the elders, by the
chief among the priests, by the scribes;* **occidi,** passive infinitive of
occidere, *to kill* (4); and *to rise* **tertia die,** ablatives, *on the third day.*
*Saying, "It is necessary that the Son of Man suffer many things and to be
rejected by the elders and chief priests and scribes and to be killed and on
the third day rise again."*

7. Luke 14:12–14

12. **Dicebat autem et ei, qui se invitaverat:**[1] **"Cum facis prandium aut cenam,**[2] **noli vocare**[3] **amicos tuos neque fratres tuos neque cognatos neque vicinos divites, ne forte et ipsi te reinvitent et fiat tibi retributio.**[4]

13. **Sed cum facis convivium,**[5] **voca pauperes, debiles, claudos, caecos;**

14. **et beatus eris,**[6] **quia non habent retribuere tibi. Retribuetur enim tibi in resurrectione iustorum."**

---

1   **Dicebat,** *he said,* imperfect indicative active; **ei,** *to him,* **qui se invitaverat:** the verb is pluperfect of **invitare** (1): **qui** refers to the one who had invited him, **se.** *But he said to him who had invited him.*

2   **Prandium, -i,** n., *lunch, late breakfast, meal;* **cena, -ae,** *banquet:* **cum facis cenam,** *when you give a banquet.*

3   **Noli** is the imperative of **nolo, nolle,** *be unwilling,* taking the infinitive **vocare,** followed by a suite of accusatives, listing ones not to invite: **amicos tuos,** *your friends,* **fratres tuos,** *your brothers,* **cognatos,** *relatives,* **vicinos divites,** *rich neighbors:* the linking **neque** = *nor.*

4   **Ne = ut non,** *in order that not, lest:* taking the subjunctives **reinvitent,** *they invite you back,* from **reinvitare** (1), *to invite back,* **fiat,** of **fio, fieri, factus sum,** the passive of **facere** (3). **Forte,** ablative of **fors, forte,** f., *chance, luck = by chance, perchance, perhaps.* **Retributio, -ionis,** f. *recompense, reward, repayment:* **et fiat tibi retributio:** *and retribution be made thee.*

5   The opposite suggestion: **convivium,** the third word for *banquet* or *meal* in the passage. **Voca,** singular imperative, making the command personal, *invite,* with a series of objects: *the poor,* **pauper, pauperis,** adjective used substantively, here in accusative plural; **debiles,** *the weak,* **claudos,** *the lame or halt,* **caecos,** *blind*—all of these adjectives used substantively.

6   **Eris,** second person singular future indicative active of **esse:** *you will be,* **beatus,** *happy.* Why? **Quia non habent retribuere tibi:** *because they have not wherewith to make recompense to you.* **Retribuetur**—the passive of the future indicative active of **retribuere** (3): when? **In resurrectione iustorum:** the ablative after **in.**

8. John 1:1–18
The Prologue

1. In principio erat Verbum, et Verbum erat apud Deum, et Deus erat Verbum.[1]

2. Hoc erat in principio apud Deum.[2]

3. Omnia per ipsum facta sunt, et sine ipso factum est nihil, quod factum est;[3]

4. in ipso vita erat, et vita erat lux hominum,[4]

5. et lux in tenebris lucet, et tenebrae eam non comprehenderunt.[5]

6. Fuit homo missus a Deo, cui nomen erat Ioannes;[6]

7. hic venit in testimonium, ut testimonium perhiberet de lumine, ut omnes crederent per illum.[7]

---

1   In principio, *in the beginning,* the ablative of principium -i, n. The verse poses no Latin problems for you.

2   hoc, the neuter demonstrative, *to agree with* verbum, -i, n. *This (word) was with the God in the beginning.*

3   Per ipsum, *through or by him,* sine ipso, *without him;* nihil = *nothing. Through him all things came to be and without him nothing that came to be came to be.*

4   Vita, -ae, f., *life;* lux, lucis, f., *light;* erat is the imperfect of esse. Hominum, is the genitive plural of homo, hominis. *In him was life, and the life was the light of men.*

5   Tenebrae, tenebrarum, *darkness;* lucet, present indicative active of lucere (2); comprehenderunt, perfect of comprehendere, *comprehend, encompass. And the light shone in darkness, and the darkness did not encompass it.*

6   Missus, past participle of mittere, *to send;* fuit, perfect of esse: *there was a man sent* a Deo, *by God;* cui nomen, *the name for whom, whose name. There was a man sent from God, whose name was John.*

7   Hic is the masculine demonstrative, to agree with John; the ut clause takes the subjunctive perhiberet from perhibere (2); the second ut, in order that, has forits object the subjunctive crederent, from

8. Non erat ille lux, sed ut testimonium perhiberet de lumine.[8]

9. Erat lux vera, quae illuminat omnem hominem, veniens in mundum.[9]

10. In mundo erat, et mundus per ipsum factus est, et mundus eum non cognovit.

11. In propria venit, et sui eum non receperunt.[10]

12. Quotquot autem acceperunt eum, dedit eis potestatem filios Dei fieri, his, qui credunt in nomine eius,[11]

13. qui non ex sanguinibus neque ex voluntate carnis neque ex voluntate viri, sed ex Deo nati sunt.[12]

14. Et Verbum caro factum est et habitavit in nobis; et vidimus gloriam eius, gloriam quasi Unigeniti a Patre, plenum gratiae et veritatis.[13]

---

credere (3) **per illum,** *through him. That all might believe through him.*

8   **lumen, -inis,** n., *light.*

9   **Mundus, -i,** m., *world;* **illuminat,** present indicative active of **illuminare** (1); **veniens,** present participle of **venire** (3), modifying **Verbum.** *He was the true light, which illumines every man coming into the world.*

10   **Propria,** neuter plural of the adjective **proprius, propria, proprium,** collectively, *his own,* **in,** *to his own;* **sui,** *his own,* **eum,** *him,* the object of the perfect **receperunt,** from **recipere** (3). *He was in the world, and the world was made by him, and the world did not know him.*

11   **Quotquot,** *however many;* **acceperunt,** *did accept or receive him,* **dedit,** perfect of **do, dare, dedi, datus,** *he gave,* **eis** *to them;* **potestatem,** accusative of **potestas, potestatis,** f., *power,* **filios Dei fieri,** *to become the sons of God,* **fieri** being a passive infinitive of **facere,** *to be made;* **qui credunt in nomine eius,** namely, *those who believe in his name. However many accepted him, to them he gave the power to become sons of God, to them that believe in his name.*

12   *How then?* **Sed ex Deo nati sunt.** Of those who believe, it is now said, by implication, **non nati sunt,** from the deponent **nascor, nasci, natus sum,** *they were not born* **ex sanguinibus, sanguis, sanguinis,** *blood,* that is, *not by a bodily birth,* **non ex voluntate carnis,** *not by the will of flesh,* nor **ex voluntate viri**—**caro, carnis,** *flesh,* **vir, viri.**

13   The Latin continues without posing difficulties for you: **factum est,** the gender explained by its agreement with **verbum; habitavit,** perfect indicative active of **habitare** (1), **in nobis,** *among us;* **vidimus,**

15. Ioannes testimonium perhibet de ipso et clamat dicens: "Hic erat, quem dixi: Qui post me venturus est, ante me factus est, quia prior me erat."[14]

16. Et de plenitudine eius nos omnes accepimus, et gratiam pro gratia;[15]

17. quia lex per Moysen data est, gratia et veritas per Iesum Christum facta est.[16]

18. Deum nemo vidit umquam; unigenitus Deus, qui est in sinum Patris, ipse enarravit.[17]

---

perfect tense, *we saw,* **gloriam eius,** *his glory.* What glory? **Gloriam quasi Unigeniti a Patri,** *the glory as of the only begotten by the Father,* **plenum gratiae et veritatis:** the adjective modifies **eum,** *him, full of grace and truth. And the word was made flesh and lived among us; and we saw his glory, the glory as of the only begotten of the Father, full of grace and truth.*

14   **Perhibet** is present indicative active, whose object is **testimonium,** *witness,* **de ipso,** *of him,* **et clamat,** another present indicative active, of **clamare** (1), *to cry out:* **Hic,** *this man* **erat** *was the one, who,* **quem, dixi,** *I said, spoke about.* **Qui post me venturus est:** *he who will come, is to come, after me;* **ante me factus est,** *came to be before me,* **quia prior me erat:** *because he was before me. John gives testimony concerning him and cries out, saying, "This was the one of whom I said: he who will come after me, came to be before me, because he was prior to me."*

15   **Accepimus,** first person plural perfect active, whose subject is **nos omnes,** *we all have received* **de plenitudine eius,** *of his plenty,* **gratia pro gratia,** *and grace for grace. And of his plenty we have all received, and grace for grace.*

16   A contrast: **lex data est:** *the law was given,* how? **Per Moysen,** *through Moses,* but **gratia et veritas,** *grace and truth,* **per Jesum Christum facta est,** *came about through Jesus Christ.*

17   **Nemo, neminis,** *no one,* **vidit,** perfect of **videre** (2) whose object is **Deum, umquam,** adverb, *ever: no man has ever seen God.* **Unigenitus Dei,** *the only begotten of God,* **qui est in sinum Patris,** *who is in the bosom of the Father*—**sinus, sinus,** m.; **ipse,** *he,* emphatic, **enarravit**—perfect of **enarrare,** *to divulge, tell, make known.*

9. John 10:7–10

7. Dixit ergo iterum Iesus: "Amen, amen, dico vobis: Ego sum ostium ovium.[1]

8. Omnes, quotquot venerunt ante me, fures sunt et latrones, sed non audierunt eos oves.[2]

9. Ego sum ostium: per me si quis introiret, salvabitur et ingredietur et egredietur et pascua invenient.[3]

10. Fur non venit, nisi ut furetur et mactet et perdat;[4] ego veni, ut vitam habeant et abundantius habeant.

---

1   **Iterum,** *again;* **ostium, -ii,** n., *the entrance, door,* **ovium,** a genitive plural, **ovis, ovis,** f., *a sheep. Again Jesus said therefore: "Amen, amen, I say to you: I am the entrance of the sheep."*

2   **Venerunt,** third person plural perfect indicative active, from **venire,** (4), *subject,* **omnes,** *all,* **quotquot,** *however many;* **fur, furis,** *thief,* **latro, latronis,** *robber:* two plurals, **fures** and **latrones; audierunt,** perfect of **audire,** *hear,* its subject is **oves,** *sheep. All, however many came before me, were thieves and robbers, but the sheep did not hear them.*

3   After **si** the subjunctive **introiret,** Christ is the entry way, and if anyone should enter through him, **salvabitur,** future passive, *he will be saved,* **ingredietur** and **egredietur,** futures of the deponents **egredior** and **ingredior,** both third conjugation, *he will go in and out,* **pascuum, -i,** n., *pasture,* **inveniet,** future of **invenire** (4), *and will find pastures. I am the entry: If anyone enters through me, he will be saved, he will go in and find pastures.*

4   **Nisi ut,** *unless that, except to,* taking the subjunctives. **furetur, mactet, perdat; furor** (1), a deponent, *to steal;* **mactare** (1), *to sacrifice;* and **perdere** (3). **Ego veni,** the perfect of **venire, ut** governing the subjunctive **habeant,** *that they might have life* et **abundantius habeant**—**abundantius** is the comparative of the adverb **abundanter,** *abundantly,* so the comparative means *more abundantly. The thief comes to steal, sacrifice and lose; I came that they might have life and have it more abundantly.*

10. Epistle to the Ephesians 4:1–6

1. Obsecro itaque vos ego vinctus in Domino, ut digne ambuletis in vocatione, qua vocati estis,[1]

2. cum omni humilitate et mansuetudine, cum longanimitate, supportantes invicem in caritate,[2]

3. solliciti[3] servare unitatem spiritus in vinculo pacis;

4. unum corpus et unus Spiritus, sicut et vocati estis in una spe vocationis vestrae;[4]

5. unus Dominus, una fides, unum baptisma;[5]

---

1 Obsecrare (1), *implore, beseech;* the subject of this verb is **ego,** modified by **vinctus,** past participle of **vincere (4),** *to conquer;* **ut,** taking the subjunctive **ambuletis,** second person plural present of **ambulare** (1), **digne,** adverb, *worthily,* **vocatione,** ablative, *in the vocation, what vocation?* **Qua vocati estis:** *in which,* an ablative, **vocati estis,** *you have been called. I beg you as one conquered in the Lord that you walk worthily in the vocation in which you were called.*

2 How? **cum omni humilitate et mansuetudine, cum longanimitate,** *with all humility, and meekness, with patience,* all ablatives with **cum,** *from,* **humilitas, humilitatis, f., mansuetudo, mansuetudinis** and **longanimitas, longanimitatis; supportantes,** nominative plural of the present participle of **supportare** (1), **invicem,** *supporting one another,* **in caritate,** *in charity.*

3 **Solliciti,** nominative plural masculine of **sollicitus, -a, -um,** *strongly moved, stirred up,* referring to **vos,** followed by the infinitive **servare** (1), *to preserve, to save,* **unitatem,** accusative of **unitas, unitatem,** *unity,* **spiritus,** fourth declension genitive, *unity of spirit,* **in vinculo pacis: vinculum, -i,** n., *bond, cord,* **pax, pacis,** f. *Moved to preserve unity of spirit in the bond of peace.*

4 **Spiritus,** fourth declension, masculine, hence **unus; corpus, corporis,** n., *one body and one spirit,* **sicut,** *just as,* **vocati estis,** *you have been called,* **in una spe,** from **spes, spei** (5), *in the one hope* **vocationis vestrae,** *of your vocation.*

5 No problem here except perhaps for **baptisma,** which looks like a

6. unus Deus et Pater omnium, qui super omnes et per omnia et in omnibus.[6]

---

feminine of the first declension, yet is modified by the neuter **unum**: it is a loan word from the Greek and neuter.

6   You should have no problems here.

Lesson Eleven
The Canticle of Zachary

WHEN ZACHARY IS ASKED what he thinks his son John will be ("**Quid putas puer iste erit?**"), he is filled with the Holy Spirit and responds with the canticle which plays such an important role in the morning prayer of the Church. We find it in Luke 1, and I will set it forth according to the verse numberings of the Gospel.

68. **Benedictus Dominus, Deus Israel,**
    quia visitavit et fecit redemptionem plebi suae
69. **et erexit cornu salutis nobis**
    in domo David pueri sui,
70. **sicut locutus est per os sanctorum,**
    qui a saeculo sunt, prophetarum eius,
71. **salutem ex inimicis nostris**
    et de manu omnium, qui oderunt nos;
72. **ad faciendum misericordiam cum patribus nostris**
    et memorari testamenti sui sancti,
73. **iusiurandum, quod iuravit ad Abraham patrem nostrum,**
    daturum se nobis,
74. **ut sine timore, de manu inimicorum liberati,**
    serviamus illi
75. **in sanctitate et iustitia coram ipso**
    omnibus diebus nostris.
76. **Et tu, puer, propheta Altissimi vocaberis:**
    praeibis enim ante faciem Domini parare vias eius,
77. **ad dandum scientiam salutis plebi eius**
    in remissionem peccatorum eorum,
78. **per viscera misericordiae Dei nostri,**
    in quibus visitabit nos oriens ex alto,
79. **illuminare his, qui in tenebris et in umbra mortis sedent,**
    ad dirigendos pedes nostros in viam pacis.

[68] Blessed be the Lord God of Israel
    because he visited and redeemed his people

[69] he has raised up the horn of salvation for us
     in the house of David his son.
[70] as he has spoken through the mouth of the saints,
     who were of old, and of his prophets,
[71] safety from our enemies
     and from the hand of all who hate us;
[72] and to be merciful with our fathers
     and to remember his holy covenant,
[73] the oath he swore to our father Abraham,
     that he would give himself for us,
[74] so that, freed from the hand of enemies,
     we might serve him without fear
[75] in holiness and justice before him
     all our days.
[76] And you, son, will be called a prophet of the most high;
     you will go before the face of the Lord to prepare his ways,
[77] to make known the salvation of his people
     in the forgiveness of their sins,
[78] through the bowels of mercy of our God
     thanks to which the rising sun will visit us
[79] to shine on those who sit in the dark and shadows of death
     to direct our feet on the way of peace.

68. **Benedictus Dominus, Deus Israel,**
quia visitavit et fecit redemptionem plebi suae

The Latin of this canticle is not easy; then again, it is not too difficult. The opening verse expressing something Zachary (or Zecheriah) wants to be so; understood is the verb *to be* in the subjunctive mood. *May the Lord God of Israel be blessed, praised.* **Visitavit** and **fecit** are third person singular in the perfect tense of their respective verbs, **visitare,** a verb of the first conjugation, and **facere,** a third conjugation verb. Their common subject is the Lord. *He visited and caused redemption for his people:* **plebi suae** is in the dative because of **fecit redemptionem,** which seems to leave **visitavit** without an object in the accusative. Either we understand **plebem suam** or take **visitare** to require an object in the dative case.

69. **et erexit cornu salutis nobis**
in domo David pueri sui,

In verse 69, **erexit** is of course the third person singular of the third conjugation verb **erigo, erigere, erexi, erectus,** *to raise or lift* *up.* **Cornu** is borrowed from the Greek and is a neuter noun meaning *horn*, as in horn of plenty or cornucopia. Thus the following genitive, **salutis**, gives: *he lifted up the horn of salvation, or plentiful salvation,* **nobis,** *for us.* **In** governs the ablative of **domus** and **David**, as the genitive **pueri** in apposition to it indicates, is in the genitive—proper nouns are not always declined, and something else must give us the clue to their case: *in the house of David his son.*

70. **sicut locutus est per os sanctorum,**
       qui a saeculo sunt, prophetarum eius,

The **locutus est** is the perfect tense of the deponent verb **loquor, loqui, locutus est.** God can speak to us indirectly, through creation, through inspired saints and prophets. Thus, **per os sanctorum,** *through the mouth of the holy ones* (**os, oris** is a neuter noun, so **os** after **per** is an accusative). **Saeculum** is a word used to signify a duration, a man's age, an age, and then takes on the sense of the English, *for ages,* meaning from the past until now. **Qui a saeculo sunt** says that the holy ones through whose mouth the Lord speaks are from old. He also speaks through the mouth of his prophets. Notice the different expressions of possession: earlier it was **plebs sua,** *his people,* and **pueri sui,** but here it is **prophetarum eius,** literally, *of the prophets of him.*

71. **salutem ex inimicis nostris**
       et de manu omnium, qui oderunt nos;

And what has he spoken? 71 tells us. **Salutem**—*safety, salvation,* in the accusative of course. *From our enemies.* **Ex** governs the ablative in the plural of the noun **inimicus** and its modifier **nostris.** **De** also governs the ablative of **manus, manu:** Whose hand are we saved from? *That of all* **omnium,** genitive plural, **qui oderunt nos,** *who hate us.*

72. **ad faciendum misericordiam cum patribus nostris**
       et memorari testamenti sui sancti,

72 gives us a gerundive expression of intention: **ad faciendam,** the Lord saves *in order to show mercy with our fathers,* literally, *to make mercy, to show pity and compassion.* **Cum** governs the ablative. What form is **memorari**? Recall the Marian prayer, the Memorare. "Remember, O most holy virgin Mary . . ." This indicates that **memorare** is an imperative. **Memorari** is a passive infinitive, that is, an infinitive in the passive voice which has an active meaning:

to remember. The verb governs the genitive, which would not surprise if we rendered **memorari** as *to be mindful of.* **Testamenti sui sancti**—*his holy testament, covenant, promise.*

73. iusiurandum, quod iuravit ad Abraham patrem nostrum, daturum se nobis

What promise or covenant? 73 begins with a striking compound **iusiurandum** whose drama seems diminished when we simply translate it as *oath.* **Iuravit** poses no problem for you: **iuro, iurare, iuravi, iuratus,** *to swear;* the third principal part is the perfect; you put it into the third person and get **iuravit:** *he swore.* **Ad Abraham patrem nostrum** poses no problems. But **daturum se nobis** certainly does. **Daturum** is the future participle of our old friend **do;** it is in the accusative, as the object of **iuravit:** *he swore that he would give* **se,** *himself,* **nobis** *for us.*

74. ut sine timore, de manu inimicorum liberati, serviamus illi

With the goal or intention or aim that **ut,** *we might serve.* Here is a subjunctive following **ut;** it is the first person plural of the third conjugation verb **servio, servire, servivi** ... *That we might serve him* **sine timore,** *without fear,* **sine** governing the ablative. But there is a clause modifying the subject of **serviamus.** We, **liberati de manu inimicorum:** *liberated,* the past participle of **libero,** a first conjugation verb, being in the nominative plural to agree with *we: freed or liberated from the hand of our enemies.*

75. in sanctitate et iustitia coram ipso omnibus diebus nostris.

75 continues the thought: that we might serve **in sanctitate et iustitia**—the meaning is clear: *in holiness and justice,* both nouns in the ablative after **in; coram** is an interesting preposition: *before* or *in the presence of* **ipso,** *him*—in the ablative after **coram.** Then the ablative phrase indicating temporal duration: **omnibus diebus nostris**—all three are plural ablatives. Their gender? No way of telling from the form and, indeed, from the noun itself, since **dies, diei,** is sometimes masculine and sometimes feminine. *For all our days* or, *all the days of our life.*

76. Et tu, puer, propheta Altissimi vocaberis: praeibis enim ante faciem Domini parare vias eius.

And now the father addresses his son. *You,* tu, *son,* **puer, vo-caberis,** *will be called.* This is the second person singular of the future passive of **vocare,** a first conjugation verb. Well, we haven't taken up the passive voice of verbs, so just take my word for it; it means *you will be called.* (Don't take my word for it. Consult the grammatical appendix for the relevant paradigm.) Called what? **Propheta Altissimi.** You will have noticed that Latin nouns do not have definite or indefinite articles; in translating into English we supply them. Should we say *a* prophet or *the* prophet? Either will do so long as the definite article is not taken exclusively as the one and only. **Altissimi**—this is a genitive of the superlative form of the adjective meaning *high.* How do we say high, higher, highest in Latin? **Altus, altior, altissimus**—and of course all of these forms are declined. Hence the masculine genitive **altissimi,** *of the most high.* Zachary continues to speak to John: **praeibis,** *you will go before.* Latin creates a great many verbs by adding prefixes; in this case, **prae,** *before.* It is added to the verb meaning *to go,* **eo ire, ivi, itus.** If you prefix that verb with **ex** you would get the participle **exitus** and the stage direction **exeunt omnes.** So John will go *before the face of the Lord;* the prefix is reinforced by the adverb **ante** meaning *before.* To do what? **Parare vias eius,** *to prepare the paths of him, or his paths.*

77. **ad dandum scientiam salutis plebi eius**
     in remissionem peccatorum eorum,

And to do more. **Ad dandum,** the gerundive of **dare,** *to give* **scientiam,** *knowledge of, or to make known,* **salutis,** the objective genitive, *knowledge of salvation;* **plebi eius. Plebi** is in the dative, since it is the indirect object of the verb, **eius** is in the genitive, the people of him = *his people.* **In remissionem peccatorum eorum**—**in** here has the sense of *for,* it governs the accusative, hence **remissionem,** followed by the genitive plural of **peccatum,** and then **eorum,** of them = *their sins.*

78. **per viscera misericordiae Dei nostri,**
     in quibus visitabit nos oriens ex alto,

Viscera has made its way into English, of course, as such and in the adjective *visceral. Through the bowels of our God's mercy*—that is how to render the first part of 78. **In quibus** *in which, by way of,* **oriens ex alto,** *the sun, the daystar, that is, Christ*—*on high,* **visitabit:** future tense third singular of the first conjugation verb **visitare,** *to visit,* **nos,** *us.*

79. illuminare his, qui in tenebris et in umbra mortis sedent,
      ad dirigendos pedes nostros in viam pacis.

The sun from on high will visit us—illuminare his, *to shine on those,*
qui sedent, *who sit* (this is a verb in the second conjugation so that
is third person plural present tense); **in tenebris,** that is the ablative
plural of **tenebrae, tenebrarum,** a plural noun which can be rendered as singular, *in the darkness,* and **in umbra** *in the shade:* **umbra,**
is a first declension noun which carried over into Italian where a
diminutive form of it is umbrella. **In tenebris et in umbra mortis,**
Christ will shine on those who sit in the darkness and shadow of death.
And then a gerundive **ad dirigendos pedes nostros:** *to direct our
feet;* notice that the verbal adjective, or gerundive, agrees with the
noun which is its object. **Pes, pedis,** is a masculine noun, **pedes** is
the accusative plural, and **nostros** agrees with it. *To direct our feet*
in viam pacis. Notice that **in** is followed by the accusative of the
first declension noun **via,** that tells us to translate it as *into,* a
directional sense, rather than just *in,* place where: *into the path* **pacis,**
of peace, the genitive of **pax.**

Reading

Here is a prayer found in the *Breviarium Romanum* that is both
good to know and a good exercise in Latin. If you drew a line
through the words we have already parsed, maybe half would
remain. The prayer has the inestimable advantage, *grammatice
loquendo,* that it includes an important construction, the ablative
absolute.

Oremus. A cunctis[1] nos, quaesumus, Domine, mentis[2] et corporis defende[3] periculis; et, intercedente beato Joseph,[4] cum

---

1   Another word, besides **omnis** and **totus** for *all:* **cunctus, cuncta,
     cunctum.** The ablative plural is called for by the preposition **a;** the
     noun modified is found just before the semicolon: **periculis.** From
     the neuter noun **periculum.** *From all perils . . .*

2   The genitive of the noun **mens, mentis** and of the noun **corpus,
     corporis,** *mind and body,* respectfully, follow on **periculis:** *of mind and
     body, defend us, Lord.*

3   No need to mention that this is an imperative of the third conjugation
     verb, **defendere.**

4   This is the first ablative absolute in the prayer. The phrase means that
     the ablatives, taken by themselves, have a peculiar role. The present
     participle of the third conjugation verb, **intercedere,** is **intercedens;**

beatis apostolis[5] tuis Petro et Paulo, atque beato Thoma[6] et omnibus Sanctis, salutem nobis tribue benignus et pacem; ut, destructis adversitatibus et erroribus universis,[7] Ecclesia tua secura
tibi serviat[8] libertate.[9] Per Christum dominum nostrum. Amen.

---

if we declined it to the ablative singular, we would get **intercedente;**
Joseph too is an ablative, as we learn from its adjective **beato.** This
ablative phrase is translated as, *blessed Joseph interceding.*

5   This ablative and its adjectives **beatis** and **tuis** and **Petro** and **Paulo**
as well as **sanctis** and its adjective **omnibus** are governed by the
prepostion **cum.** *With your blessed apostles Peter and Paul . . .*

6   The prayer has *N.* here, standing for **nomen,** *name,* meaning you can
insert any saint's name you wish. I of course put in Thomas Aquinas
(Thomas the apostle already being invoked along with the other ten):
and blessed Thomas and all the saints.

7   Here is another ablative absolute. **Destructis** is the plural absolute
of the participle of the third conjugation verb, **destruere.** It governs
two ablative plurals, that of the noun **adversitas** and that of the noun
error, erroris, both modified by **universis,** yet another word for all.
How to translate the phrase? *Grant us, benignant one, salvation and*
peace, so that all adversities and errors being destroyed . . .

8   Subjunctive because the phrase is introduced by **ut.**

9   An ablative of manner—*in freedom: . . . your church made secure may*
serve you in freedom.

Lesson Twelve

The Canticle of Simeon

LUKE'S GOSPEL HAS BEEN THE SOURCE of many of the texts on which we have based lessons in this introductory course on ecclesiastical Latin. The visitation of the Angel provides us with the opening of the **Ave Maria** and Elizabeth's greeting when her cousin Mary visits continues the prayer. And Mary bursts forth with her great prayer of thanksgiving, the **Magnificat**. Then, when the birth of John the Baptist is narrated, his father Zachary, his tongue loosed, provides us with the great prayer, the **Benedictus Dominus, Deus Israel**. And next, after the birth of Jesus, when the Incarnate God is brought to the temple, the aged Simeon, recognizing that the prophecy of the coming of the Messiah has been fulfilled in Jesus, utters a moving valedictory prayer, which is always used in the night prayer of the Church. For that reason, I append the antiphon that accompanied it in Compline.

The Latin, you will see, is quite simple. Before going on, identify the nouns, verbs and adjectives of the canticle.

1. **Nunc dimittis servum tuum, Domine, secundum verbum tuum in pace.**
2. **Quia viderunt oculi mei salutem tuam,**
3. **Quam parasti ante faciem omnium populorum,**
4. **Lumen ad revelationem gentium et gloriam plebis tuae Israel.**

Salva nos, Domine, vigilantes, custodi nos dormientes; ut vigilemus cum Christo, et requiescamus in pace.

[1] Now do you dismiss your servant, Lord, according to your word in peace.
[2] Because my eyes have seen your salvation.
[3] Which you prepared before the face of all peoples,
[4] A light for the revelation of the gentiles and the glory of your people, Israel.

Lord, save us who are keeping vigil, watch over us while we are sleeping, that we might keep vigil with Christ and rest in peace.

A beautiful prayer which, as we read in Luke, Simeon spoke while he held the infant Jesus in his arms. It is a dramatic scene in which this ancient holy Jew recognizes that what has been promised to Israel has come and will be a revelation for all nations.

1. **Nunc dimittis servum tuum, Domine.** The adverb **nunc,** *now,* underscores the importance of the moment. **Dimittis** you will recognize as the second person singular of **dimitto, dimittere, dimisi, dimissus:** *you dismiss.* Its object is the noun **servum,** masculine singular accusative, modified by **tuum:** *thy servant.* **Domine** is in the vocative: the Lord is being addressed.

* **secundum verbum tuum in pace.** The word **secundum** may look like the cardinal number, second, but it is actually formed from one of those deponent verbs, **sequor, sequi, secutus sum,** and means *following,* or *according to.* (When you think about it, the ordinal number *second* is the number following on the first, which is doubtless its etymological origin.) *According to* **verbum tuum,** the word *word* in the accusative along with its adjective. **In pace**—*in peace.* This phrase could be rendered: *peacefully, as you promised.*

2. **Quia viderunt oculi mei salutem tuam.** No problems here. The sentence begins with **quia,** *because,* and then, rearranging, we identify **oculi mei** as the subject. The plural of the masculine noun **oculus,** since it is second declension, is **oculi,** and the possessive adjective, **mei,** will agree with the noun in gender number and case, hence **mei.** The verb you immediately recognize as third person plural and in the perfect tense of **video, videre, vidi, visus.** And what have Simeon's old eyes seen? **Salutem tuam:** *your salvation.*

(The third principal part of **video** may stir a memory. **Veni, vidi, vici,** Caesar said: *I came, I saw, I conquered.* The Church uses, remember, the Italian pronunciation, so the *v*'s sound as they do in English . . . or Italian. You may have heard it as "Wayney, weedy, weechie," the pronunciation preferred by classicists but which, to the Catholic ear, sounds oddly.)

3. **Quam parasti ante faciem omnium populorum.** The relative pronoun with which this verse begins refers back to **salutem,** and that is why it is feminine singular: and accusative as the object of **parasti,** second person singular of the perfect of **paro, parare, paravi, paratus,** *the salvation you have prepared.* The next phrase is a biblical metaphor: **ante faciem,** *before the face* or *in the presence of,* **omnium**

populorum, the genitive plural of the neuter noun **populum,** modified by the genitive plural of **omnis, omnis, omne,** so: *of all the peoples. Which you have prepared in the presence of all the peoples.*

4. **Lumen ad revelationem gentium, et gloriam plebis tuae Israel.** *A light,* **lumen, luminis,** a neuter noun, *a light,* **ad revelationem gentium; ad** is a preposition governing the accusative, for the revelation, **gentium,** from **gens, gentis,** a noun whose nominative plural is **gentes,** and of which we have here its genitive plural, *of the nations, of the gentiles; and the glory,* **gloriam,** the accusative singular of **gloria.** This alerts us to the fact that **lumen** is accusative, not nominative (though the two forms are the same for a neuter noun) and that both are the objects of **viderunt,** what the eyes of Simeon have seen. **Plebis** is the genitive singular of the noun **plebs** which, as its adjective **tuae** makes clear, is feminine. So Simeon's eyes have also seen: *a light for the revelation of the gentiles and the glory of thy people Israel.*

The antiphon employs the deprecative imperative of **salvo, salvare, salvavi, salvatus** and of the fourth conjugation verb, **custodio, custodire, custodivi, custoditus. Salva nos** and **custodi nos.** We pray that God may keep us safe and take care of us, both **vigilantes** and **dormientes.** Now these are present participles, used adjectively, and modifying **nos**—as we are keeping watch and as we are sleeping. There follows a phrase introduced by **ut,** in order that; this is always a signal that the verb to follow will be in the subjunctive mood. We have concentrated up until now on verbs in the indicative mode. But when a phrase is introduce by *in order that,* the verb which follows will express, not what is, but what might be. **Vigelemus** and **requiescamus** are both third person plural subjunctives—*that we might keep watch and that we might rest,* but also that we might watch **cum Christo,** *with Christ,* and *that we might rest* **in pace,** *in peace.* A fitting prayer after the recitation of the Canticle of Simeon.

Present Subjunctive Active of the Five Conjugations

Person	1	2	3	4	5
			Singular		
1st	amem	moneam	regam	capiam	audiam
2nd	ames	moneas	regas	capias	audias
3rd	amet	moneat	regat	capiat	audiat

	1	2	3	4	5
Person		*Plural*			
1st	amemus	moneamus	regamus	capiamus	audiamus
2nd	ametis	moneatis	regatis	capiatis	audiatis
3rd	ament	moneant	regant	capiant	audiant

Perfect Subjunctive Active of the Five Conjugations

	1	2	3	4	5
Person			*Singular*		
1st	amaverim	monuerim	rexerim	ceperim	audiverim
2nd	amaveris	monueris	rexeris	ceperis	audiveris
3rd	amaverit	monuerit	rexerit	ceperit	audiverit

			Plural		
1st	amaverimus	monuerimus	rexerimus	ceperimus	audiverimus
2nd	amaveritis	monueritis	rexeritis	ceperitis	audiveritis
3rd	amaverint	monuerint	rexerint	ceperint	audiverint

Translation of the present is easy: *I may love, you may love, she may love, we may love, you may love, they may love.* For the perfect, see the grammatical appendix. There are various syntactical clues, such as **ut,** that the subjunctive follows.

Reading

Here is another prayer from the night office. Try your hand at translating it into English. Some helps and hints are appended.

Oremus.[1] **Visita,**[2] **quaesumus,**[3] **Domine, habitationem istam, et omnes insidias**[4] **inimici ab ea longe**[5] **repelle:**[6] **Angeli tui sancti**

---

1   This is from **oro, orare, oravi, oratus,** and in the subjunctive. *Let us pray.*

2   Imperative from **visito,** a first conjugation verb. *Visit, we beseech, Lord, this house . . .*

3   From third conjugation verb **quaeso.**

4   Accusative plural of first declension noun **insidia:** *and drive far from it all the deceits of the enemy.*

5   This is an adverb meaning *a long way, far off.*

6   Another imperative.

habitent[7] in ea, qui nos in pace custodiant;[8] et benedictio tua sit[9] super nos semper.[10]

---

7   Subjunctive from first conjugation verb **habito:** *may they dwell: may your holy angels dwell in it.*

8   Another subjunctive. *And keep us in peace.*

9   This is the present subjunctive of the verb *to be:* **sim, sis, sit, simus, sitis, sint.** *And your blessing be always upon us.*

10   If you don't know this word, ask a Marine.

Homilia Sancti Ambrosii

In Evangelium secundum Lucam

Quae sunt ista verae fidei munera?[1] Aurum Regi, thus Deo, myrrha defuncto.[2] Aliud enim Regis insigne, aliud divinae sacramentum potestatis, aliud honor est sepulturae, quae non corrumpat corpus mortui, sed reservet.[3] Nos quoque, qui haec audimus et legimus, de thesauris nostris talia, fratres, munera proferamus.[4] Habemus enim thesaurum in vasis fictilibus.[5] Si igitur in teipso quod es, non ex te debes aestimare, sed ex Christo: quanto magis in Christo non tua debes aestimare, sed Christi?[6]

---

1 **Munus, -eris,** n. *gift;* the nominative neuter plural answers to the gender, number, and case of **quae,** the interrogative pronoun: *What are the gifts of true faith?* How do you know the gender of **fides, fidei?**

2 These are the gifts of the Magi: gold, frankincense, and myrrh: **aurum, -i,** n. *gold;* **regi** is the dative singular of **rex, regis,** m. **Thus, thuris,** n., *incense, for God,* **Deo. Myrhha defuncto**—*for the dead.*

3 **Aliud . . . aliud . . . aliud:** *the one . . . the other . . . the other.* Gold is the sign of the king. **Insigne, -is,** n, *token, sign.* Incense is the **potestatis sacramentum divinae:** *the sacrament of divine power.* **Potestas, -tatis,** f. (3). **Corrumpare** (1) has as its object **corpus,** the accusative of **corpus, -oris,** n. (3), followed by the genitive **mortui** from **mortuum, -ui,** n. **Reservet** is from **reservare** (1) and is present subjunctive active.

4 **Quoque,** *too, also;* **talia munera,** nominative plural accusatives, *such like gifts,* the object of **proferamus:** subjunctive, *may we offer.* **Nos qui audimus et legimus:** two present tenses: *we too who hear and read.* **Fratres,** vocative plural of **frater, fratris,** m. (3). **Thesaurum, -i,** n., *treasury. May we too, brothers, who hear and read these things, offer similar gifts from our own treasures.*

5 Can you place the Pauline allusion? **In vasis fictilibis. Fictilis, fictile,** adj., *earthen, made of clay.* **Vas, vasis,** n., *vessel.*

6 **Debes** from **debere** (2), indicative present despite the **si.** *If therefore you ought not reckon what is in yourself as from yourself, but from Christ . . .* **Quanto magis:** *how much more you should esteem as of Christ, not yours.* **Aestimare** is first conjugation.

Ergo Magi de thesauris suis offerunt munera.[7] Vultis scire quam bonum meritum habeant?[8] Stella ab his videtur: ubi Herodes est, non videtur; ubi Christus est, rursus videtur, et viam demonstrat.[9] Ergo stella haec via est, et via Christus: quia secundum incarnationis mysterium Christus est stella.[10] Orietur[11] enim stella ex Jacob, et exsurget homo ex Israel. Denique ubi Christus, et stella est. Ipse enim est stella splendida et matutina.[12] Sua igitur ipse luce se signat.[13]

Accipe aliud documentum.[14] Alia venerunt via Magi, alia redeunt.[15] Qui enim Christum viderant, Christum intellexerant;[16] meliores utique, quam venerant, revertuntur. Duae quippe sunt viae: una, quae ducit ad interitum; alia, quae ducit ad regnum.[17]

---

7   Offerunt from **offero, offerre, obtuli, oblatus** (3), from which *oblation* also comes. *Therefore the Magi offer gifts from their own treasuries.*

8   Ambrose is still addressing his brothers. Hence **vultis** from **volo, velle, volui, vultus**, so this is second person plural perfect active: **quam bonum meritum:** *what good merit*, the object of **habeant**, the present subjunctive of **habere**, (2) *to have. You wanted to know what good merit they might have?*

9   Ambrose points out what the Magi had that Herod did not: **stella, -ae**, *star*, **ab his videtur:** *it was seen by them:* **ubi Herodes est, non videtur; ubi** = *where. The star was visible again where Christ was:* **ubi Christus est, rursus videtur. Rursus.** again: **et viam demonstrat. Demonstrare** is first conjugation, this is third person singular present indicative active, and its object is the accusative of **via, -ae**, f., *way.*

10   *The star is the way, Christ is the way; Christ is the star;* **secundum incarnationis mysterium,** *according to the mystery of the incarnation.*

11   Ambrose continues this thought. **Orietur** from the deponent **orior, oriri, ortus sum** (4), it is third person singular of the future indicative passive. **Exsurgere** (3) is also future.

12   **Splendida**, *shining*, modifying **stella**, as does **matutina**, *morning.*

13   **Ipse**, *he*, is the subject; the verb is **signat**, from **signare** (1), *to mark or designate*, and its object is the reflexive **se** and **luce**, the ablative of **lux, lucis**, f. **Igitur** = *therefore. Therefore he designates or makes himself known by his own light.*

14   **Accipe** is an imperative from **accipere** (3); **documentum, -i**, n. *example, warning, proof*, modified by **aliud** the neuter of **alius, alia, aliud**, *other, another.*

15   **Via** and its repeated modifier **alia**, are ablative; **reddeunt** is from **reddeo, reddere** (2).

16   Both **intellexerant** and **viderant** are pluperfect. **Melius**, comparative of **bonus. Utique**, adv.: *in any case, at any rate, certainly. Those who saw Christ understood him better when they returned than when they arrived.*

Illa peccatorum est, quae ducit ad Herodem; haec Christus est, qua reditur ad patriam.[18] Hic enim temporalis est incolatus sicut scriptum est: Multum incola facta est anima mea.[19]

---

17   **Quippe,** conj., *indeed;* **ducit** from **ducere** (3); **interitus, -us,** m. (4), *destruction;* **regnum, -i,** n. *the kingdom.*

18   **Illa . . . haec:** *the former (way), the latter (way);* **qua,** is an ablative, *by which or whereby;* **reditur** from **redire** (2), future passive indicative. **Patria, -ae.** f. *fatherland, homeland, heaven.*

19   **Incolo, incolere, incolui, incultum** (3), *inhabit, dwell in;* **incolatus** is a dwelling place: as opposed to **patria,** *we have here a temporal dwelling place. My soul has become an inhabitant*—**multum** seems adverbial, *much,* or *often.*

Saint Augustine (1)

Lectio Sancti Evangelii
Secundum Ioannem, 15, 17–25

In illo tempore dixit Iesus discipulis suis:[1] Haec mando vobis, ut diligatis invicem.[2] Si mundus vos odit, scitote quia me priorem vobis odio habuit. Et reliqua.[3]

Homilia sancti Augustini Episcopi, Tractatus 87, in Ioannem.

In lectione evangelica quae hanc antecedit, dixerat Dominus: Non vos me elegistis; sed ego elegi vos et posuit vos, ut eatis, et fructum afferatis, et fructus vester maneat: ut quodcumque petieritis Patrem in nomine meo, det vobis.[4] Hic autem dicit: Haec mando vobis, ut diligatis invicem. Ac per hoc intelligere debemus hunc esse fructum nostrum, de quo ait: Ego vos elegi, ut eatis, et fructum afferatis, et fructus vester maneat. Et quod adjunxit, Ut quodcumque petieritis Patrem in nomine meo, det vobis, tunc utique dabit nobis, si diligimus invicem; cum et hoc ipsum ipse dederit nobis, qui nos elegit non habentes fructum,[5]

---

1   A familiar Gospel locution: *At that time Jesus said to his disciples.* **Discipulis** is dative plural of **discipulus.**

2   **Invicem**—*by turns, alternately.* Here it means *one another. This I command you, that you love one another.* **Oremus pro invicem** is a familiar phrase: *let us pray for one another.*

3   An alternative to **et caetera.** This refers to the remainder of the Gospel passage Augustine is preaching about.

4   There are many subjunctives here, governed by the two occurrences of **ut,** *in order that. You did not choose me,* Christ says, *but I chose and placed you.* Why? **ut eatis . . . afferatis . . . maneat:** *that you might go, might bear fruit and that your fruit might endure or remain. And in order that whatever you might ask*—**petieritis**—*the Father in my name,* **det vobis**—*he might give you.*

5   That is, Christ did not choose us because we deserved; nor did we

quia non eum nos elegeramus, et posuit nos ut fructum affera-
mus, hoc est invicem diligamus.

Caritas ergo est fructus noster, quam definit Apostolus, De
corde puro, et conscientia bona, et fide non ficta.[6] Hac diligimus
invicem, hac diligimus Deum; neque enim vera dilectione dilig-
eremus invicem, nisi diligentes Deum. Diligit enim unusquisque proximum suum tamquam seipsum, si diligit Deum, Nam,
si non diligit Deum, non diligit seipsum; in his enim duobus
praeceptis caritatis tota lex pendet et prophetae. Hic est fructus
noster. De fructu itaque nobis mandans, Haec mando, inquit, ut
diligatis invicem. Unde et Apostolus Paulus, cum contra opera
carnis commendare fructum spiritus vellet, a capite hoc posuit:
Fructus, inquit, spiritus, caritas est; ac deinde cetera, tamquam ex
isto capite exorta et religata contexuit, quae sunt, gaudium, pax,
longanimitas, benignitas, bonitas, fides, mansuetudo, continentia, castitas.[7]

Quis autem bene gaudet, qui bonum non diligit unde gaudet?[8]
Quis pacem veram, nisi cum illo potest habere, quem veraciter
diligit? Quis est longanimis in bono opere perseveranter ma-
nendo, nisi ferveat diligendo? Quis est benignus, nisi diligat cui
opitulatur?[9] Quis bonus nisi diligendo efficiatur? Quis salubriter

---

choose him: **elegeramus** = parse this occurrence of **eligere**.

6   *Charity is our fruit, which Paul defines as from a pure heart and a good*
       conscience and unaffected faith = **non ficta:** *not pretended.*

7   The way Augustine turns the Scriptural passages over and over
       keeps the vocabulary small even while the thought deepens. You will
       no doubt be delightfully surprised at how easily you follow the Latin
       text. Only a few verbs and nouns and constructions are in play. Of
       course, your familiarity with the Gospel and with Paul explains this
       in part.
            By this we love one another, by this we love God; for neither do we love
       one another with a true love unless loving God. One will love his neighbor
       as himself if he loves God. For if he does not love God, he does not love himself;
       for on these two precepts of charity depend the whole law and the prophets.
       This is our fruit. He said, "This I command, that you love one another."
       Hence the Apostle Paul, when he wishes to commend the fruit of the spirit
       against the works of the flesh, puts this at the head: "The fruit of the spirit
       in charity," he said; and then the rest as arising from this head. . . .

8   *Who can rejoice well who does not love the good whence (because of which)*
       he rejoices? The series of questions derives from the marks of the spirit
       of charity Augustine has found enumerated in Paul: joy, peace,
       longsuffering, benignity, goodness, faith, meekness, continence, and
       chastity.

9   From the deponent verb **opitulor** = *to help. Salubriter* = *healthily,*

fidelis, nisi ea fide quae per dilectionem efficiatur? Quis utiliter
mansuetus, cui non dilectio moderetur? Quis ab eo continet unde
turpatur, nisi diligat unde honestatur?[10] Merito itaque[11] Magister
bonus dilectionem sic saepe commendat, tamquam sola praecipi-
enda sit, sine qua non possunt prodesse cetera bona, et quae non
potest haberi sine ceteris bonis, quibus homo efficitur bonus.

[Rom Brev. Oct 28]

---

wholesomely.

10   The verb here goes back to **continentia,** *moderation. Who can be
     continent with respect to that by which he might be defiled, unless he loves
     that whence he is made virtuous?*

11   *Rightly therefore:* **merito** *is an adverb;* **itaque** *is literally and so.* **Saepe**
     = *often. Rightly therefore the good Master often commends love thus, as if
     it alone were commanded, without which the other goods cannot come forth,
     and which cannot be had without the other goods, whereby a man is made
     good.*

Saint Augustine (2)

Homilia Sancti Augustini

Lectio sancti Evangelii secundum Matthaeum 6:24–33

In illo tempore: Dixit Jesus discipulis suis: Nemo potest duobus dominis servire. Et reliqua.

Nemo potest duobus dominis[1] servire. Ad hanc ipsam intentionem referendum est[2] quod consequenter exponit, dicens: Aut enim unum odio habebit, et alterum diliget; aut alterum patietur, et alterum contemnet.[3] Quae verba diligenter consideranda sunt:[4] nam qui sint duo domini, deinceps[5] ostendit, cum dicit: Non potestis Deo servire, et mammonae. Mammona apud Hebraeos divitiae appelari dicuntur.[6] Congruit[7] et Punicum nomen; nam lucrum Punice mammon dicitur.

Sed qui servit mammonae, illi utique servit,qui rebus istis

---

1   Servire takes the dative, hence duobus dominis.

2   Here is a gerund, referendum est, *ought to be referred;* to what? Ad hanc ipsam intentionem: *to this very intention.* As to what ought to be referred to that intention, it is quod consequenter exponit: *what he goes on to say or explain.* Exponere is third conjugation.

3   Aut ... aut, *either or.* Habebit and diliget future tenses; odio habere, *to hold in hate, to hold in contempt, to hate;* patietur and contemnet are also in the future tense.

4   Here is a nice gerundive phrase: quae verba diligenter consideranda sunt: *which words should be diligently considered.* Consideranda is neuter plural—the gerundive is a verbal adjective and is declined to agree with verba; the adverb suggests 'lovingly.' Why?

5   This adverb means *one after another, successively;* so as to *what,* qui, *these* duo domini, *two masters,* sint, *might be,* he shows one after another—perhaps even next—cum dicit, when he says ...

6   Mammon is used as synonymous with divitiae, *riches:* and Augustine tells us the word was borrowed from the Punic, in which language it means lucrum, -i, n. *gain, profit, advantage.*

7   From congruere (3), *to coincide, to correspond.*

terrenis merito suae perversitatis praepositus, magistratus hujus saeculi a Domino dicitur.[8] Aut enim unum odio habebit homo, et alterum diliget, id est, Deum; aut alterum patietur, et alterum contemnet. Patietur[9] enim durum et perniciosum dominum, quisquis[10] servit mammonae; sua enim cupiditate implicatus, subditur diabolo, et non eum diligit. Quis enim est qui diligat diabolum? sed tamen patitur.

Ideo inquit,[11] dico vobis, non habere sollicitudinem animae vestrae quid edatis,[12] neque corpori vestro quid induatis; ne forte, quamvis jam superflua non quaerantur, propter ipsa necessaria cor duplicetur, et ad ipsa conquirenda, nostra detorqueatur intentio,[13] cum aliquid quasi misericorditer operamur; id est, ut cum consulere alicui videri volumus, nostrum emolumentum ibi

---

8 The thoughts are rapidly juxtaposed: **sed qui servit mammonae—** *but who serves Mammon?* **illi utique,** *those indeed,* **merito,** *as a punishment* (**meritum, -i,** n., *desert, reward*), **suae perversitatis,** *of their perversity,* **qui praepositus rebus istis terrenis,** *who have set before themselves these earthly things,* ablative because of the prefix **prae** in the compound word, **dicitur a Domino,** *called by the Lord,* **magistratus hujus saeculi:** *the prince of this world.*

9 Augustine now explains the word he has quoted: *he will suffer one master and contemn the other.* Why **patietur?** *One who serves Mammon suffers a hard and pernicious master:* **implicatus sua cupiditate,** *caught by his own greed*—**cupiditas, cupiditatis,** f.—**subditur diabolo: subdere** (3), *to set under,* and our verb here is passive, *is set under the devil. For who could love the devil?* **Quis est qui**—*who is it who,* **diligat,** subjunctive since **diligere** is third conjugation, as a check of the paradigms in the back of the book will confirm.

10 **quisquis, quaequae, quidquid,** *whoever, whichever.*

11 **Inquit,** he says, from a defective verb with only a few forms; it is however quite familiar in this form; **itaque,** *and so, therefore.*

12 From **edo, edere, edi, esus** (1), *to eat,* second person plural present indicative active; **induere** (3), *to put on, to wear;* **corpori vestro,** *what you wear on your body.*

13 Augustine here suggests a subtler way of serving Mammon which can follow on concern for what we eat or what we wear. **Ne,** *lest,* **forte,** *perhaps,* **jam superflua non quaerantur**—*not now the superfluous, that which beyond need, is sought,* yet **propter ipsa necessaria,** *because of those necessities*—**necessarium -i,** n.—**cor duplicetur,** *the heart might be divided*—the subjunctive after **ne: et ad ipsa conquirenda,** *in seeking to conquer them*—**nostra intentio detorqueatur:** from **detorquere** (2), *to turn away,* here passive present subjunctive, *might be turned away, even when we do something as if mercifully,* **cum aliquid quasi misericorditer operamur** (a first conjugation deponent, **operor**).

potius, quam illius utilitatem attendamus; et ideo nobis non
videamur peccare, quia non superflua, sed necessaria sint, quae
consequi volumus.[14]

---

14   His example is a Gospel one. **Ut cum,** *as when,* **volumus,** *we wish,*
     videri, *to be seen,* a passive infinitive, **consulere,** (3), *to advise,* **alicui,**
     someone, a dative; **nostrum emolumentum,** *our reward,* is **potius ibi,**
     rather there, **quam attendamus,** *than that we attend to,* **illius utilitatem,**
     his benefit or utility. **Et ideo non videamur:** *and therefore we are not seen,*
     that is, *we do not seem,* **peccare** (1), *to sin,* **quia,** *because,* **quae volumus**
     consequi, *what we wish to go after*—**consequi,** is the infinitive of the
     deponent **consequor** (3), *are not luxuries,* **superflua,** *but necessities,*
     necessaria sunt.

Lesson Sixteen

Sermo Sancti Bedae Venerabilis Presbyteri

In festo Omnium Sanctorum die 1 Nov.
Sermo 18 de Sanctis

Hodie dilectissimi,[1] omnium sanctorum sub una solemnitatis laetitia celebramus[2] festivitatem; quorum[3] societate caelum exsultat, quorum patrociniis terra laetatur, triumphis Ecclesia sancta coronatur. Quorum confessio quanto in passione fortior, tanto[4] est clarior in honore; quia, dum crevit pugna, crevit[5] et pugnantium gloria, et martyrii triumphus multiplici passionum genere[6] adornatur, perque[7] graviora tormenta, graviora fuere[8] et

---

1   This is the superlative of **dilecti,** the vocative plural; *most beloved.* Later, Venerable Bede will address his listeners as **carissimi,** *most dear or beloved.* The superlative of the vocative **caro.**

2   *We celebrate the feast of all the saints under the joy of one observance.*

3   The first of several occurrences of **quorum,** referring to all the saints: *in the society of whom, heaven rejoices, in whose protection the earth is made joyful, by whose triumphs the holy Church is crowned.* **Patrocinium** is a neuter noun of which the ablative plural is found here: *by protections,* literally, or, *by defenses.*

4   **Quanto . . . tanto**: this locution signals a comparison. *Whose confessing [of the faith] the stronger it was in suffering, the brighter it is in honor.* **Fortior** is the comparative of the adjective **fortis,** and **clarior** the comparative of **clarus**—forms required when a comparison is being made—needless to say, he said, saying it.

5   Third person singular of the perfect active of **cresco, crescere, crevi, cretus,** *to grow up, arise, increase. When the struggle,* **pugna,** *the fight, increased, the glory of the struggling also increased.* **Pugnantium** is the genitive plural of the present participle of the first conjugation verb **pugnare. Pugna** is a first declension noun from the same stem.

6   *The triumph of the martyr is adorned by many kinds of sufferings.* **Genere** is the ablative singular of **genus, generis,** a noun whose link with generation is obvious, which is why a first meaning of the word is clan or race; then it is extended to any kind of classificatory schema.

7   Bede could have said **et per,** but your ear will tell you that **perque** is preferable; the enclitic **-que** you remember = **et. Adornatur**: a third person singular passive of **adornare** (1), whose subject is **triumphus, -i,** m.

praemia. Dum catholica mater Ecclesia, quae per totum orbem[9] longe lateque diffusa est, in ipso capite suo Christo Jesu edocta est contumelias, cruces et mortem non timere;[10] magis magisque[11] roborata, non resistendo sed perferendo, universis, quos agmine inclyto carcer poenalis inclusit, pari et simile calore virtutis, ad gerendum certamen, gloriam triumphalem inspiravit.

O vere[12] beata mater Ecclesia, quam sic honor divinae dignationis illuminat, quam vincentium, gloriosus Martyrum sanguis exornat, quam inviolatae confessionis candida induit virginitas! Floribus ejus nec rosae nec lilia desunt.[13] Certent nunc, carissimi, singuli ut ad utrosque honores amplissimam accipiant dignitatem, coronas vel de virginitate candidas vel de passione purpureas.[14] In caelestibus castris pax et acies habent flores suos, quibus milites Christi coronantur.[15]

---

8   This is a form of **fuerunt** = third person plural of the perfect of **esse** = *they,* that is, *the torments, were:* but as with the **quanto . . . tanto** above, the meaning is: *the greater were the torments, the greater were the rewards.*

9   Throughout the world. **Orbis, orbis,** feminine = *the orb.* The phrase **orbs terrarum** is often used for global comprehensiveness. **Longe lateque** = *far and wide,* both ablatives of manner or extent become adverbs.

10   *The Church, spread far and wide throughout the world, has been taught by its head Jesus Christ not to fear insolence, crosses and death.*

11   Repetition for emphasis = *far rather.* **Agmen, agminis** = *throng;* **inclytus, inclyta, inclytum,** *celebrated, famous.* **Carcer, carceris** = *prison.* **Certamen, certaminis** = *contest, struggle.*

12   An adverb = *truly, indeed. O blessed mother Church, which the honor of the divine favor thus illumines, which the blood of the conquering, glorious martyrs adorns, which the snowwhite virginity of the testimony of the unviolated clothes!* **Dignatio, -onis,** f. modified by **divinae,** both the objective genitive after **honor, -is,** the subject of **illuminat,** from **illuminare** (1).

13   The verb is formed of **de** and **esse** and means to lack. So: *neither roses nor lilies are missing from its flowers.*

14   Bede now exhorts his hearer. **Certent** is subjunctive, third person plural, of **certare.** Its subject is **singuli** = *let all now struggle that they might receive both honors and the fullest dignity, either the dazzling crowns of virginity or the purple of suffering.*

15   Bede continues the metaphor of Christian combat, familiar at least since Paul and Augustine. *In the heavenly camp peace and the army will have their own flowers (rewards), whereby the soldiers of Christ are crowned.* **Castrum, -i,** n., (2) *fort* or *camp;* **acies, -ei,** f., *army;* **miles, militis,** *soldier;* **coronantur** is the third person present passive of **coronare** (1).

Dei enim ineffabilis et immensa bonitas etiam hoc providit, ut laborum quidem tempus et agonis non extenderet noc longum faceret aut aeternum, sed breve et, ut ita dicam, momentaneum:[16] ut in hic brevi et exigua vita agones essent et labores, in illa vero quae aeterna est, coronae et praemia meritorum; ut labores quidem cito finirentur, meritorum vero praemia sine fine durarent; ut post hujus mundi tenebras visuri essent candidissimam lucem, et accepturi majorem passionum beatitudinem, testante hoc idem Apostolo, ubi ait:[17] Non sunt condignae passiones hujus temporis ad superventuram gloriam, quae revelabitur in nobis.

---

16   A single extended thought to proclaim that the trials of this life are brief and compared to eternity of little account. *The ineffable and enormous goodness of God has so provided that the time of works and struggle is not long or endless, but short and, if I may say so, momentary: in order that in this brief and tiny life there might be struggles and efforts, but in that eternal (life) the crowns and rewards of merits.* **Cito** = *quickly, swiftly.* **Visuri essent** and **accepturi essent** are future subjunctives: *in order that after the shadows of this world they will have seen the brightest light and will receive a happiness greater that all their bitter sufferings.* **Majorem** here is followed by the genitive of comparison.

17   Paul says that the sufferings of this time are not on the same level— **condignae**—*of the same worth, as the glory that is to come, which will be revealed in us.* **Agonis, -is,** *struggle,* plural **agones; testante hoc idem Apostolo,** an ablative absolute, **testante** being the ablative singular of the present participle of **testare** (1), *giving witness: the Apostle testifying to this same thing.*

Lesson Seventeen

Saint Bernard of Clairvaux
Sermo Sancti Bernardi Abbatis
In Festo Septem Dolorum B.M.V.

Martyrium Virginis tam[1] in Simeonis prophetia, quam in ipsa Dominicae passionis historia commendatur. Positus est hic (ait sanctus senex de puero Jesu)[2] in signum cui contradicetur; et tuam ipsius animam (ad Mariam autem dicebat) pertransibit gladius.[3] Vere tuam, o beata Mater, animam pertransivit. Alioquin non nisi eam pertransiens, carnem Filii tui penetraret.[4] Et quidem posteaquam emisit spiritum tuus ille Jesus, ipsius plane non attigit animam crudelis lancea, quae ipsius aperuit latus, sed tuam utique animam pertransivit.[5] Ipsius nimirum anima jam ibi non erat, sed tua plane inde nequibat avelli.[6]

---

1   **Tam . . . quam:** correlatives, *both . . . and;* **commendare** (1), *is commended to our attention. The martyrdom of the Virgin is commended both in the prophecy of Simeon and in the very story of the Lord's passion.*

2   St. Bernard refers to the **Nunc dimittis. Senex** is an adjective whose comparative is **senior,** *old, older;* it is used here substantively: *the holy old man speaks of the boy Jesus.*

3   **Pertransire,** *to pass through, to pierce;* **gladius -i,** m, *sword;* **in signum cui contradicetur:** *for a sign, which will be contradicted.*

4   Bernard addresses Mary directly. *O blessed Mother, truly it pierced your soul.* **Alioquin,** *otherwise:* Bernard makes the piercing of Mary's heart the precondition of the piercing of her son's flesh. **Non nisi eam pertransiens:** *not unless piercing it,* the present participle of **pertransire** (4): **penetraret,** is subjunctive in the imperfect of **penetrare** (1).

5   **Tuus ille Jesus,** *your Jesus:* **posteaquam,** *after, later,* **emisit,** *he sent forth* **spiritum:** that is, died. **Emittere** (3). **Lancea,** *the spear,* **crudelis,** *cruel,* **non attigit,** perfect from **attingere** (3) **animam ipsius,** *his soul,* **plane,** adverb: *Plainly the cruel lance did not attain his soul,* **quae ipsius latus aperuit,** *which opened his side;* **sed pertransivit,** *but it pierced,* **tuam animam,** *your soul.*

6   **Avellere** (3), *to tear away,* **avelli** is a passive infinitive; **nequeo, nequere, nequivi, nequitus,** (4) *to be unable;* **nimirum,** adv., *doubtless, truly. His soul was then clearly no longer there, but plainly yours was unable to be torn away from there.*

Tuam ergo pertransivit animam vis doloris,[7] ut plusquam
Martyrem non immerito praedicemus, in qua nimirum corporeae
sensum passionis excesserit compassionis affectus. An non tibi
plusquam gladius fuit sermo ille, revera pertransiens animam, et
pertingens usque ad divisionem animae et spiritus: Mulier, ecce
filius tuus?[8] O commutationem![9] Joannes tibi pro Jesu traditur,
servus pro Domino, discipulus pro Magistro, filius Zebedaei pro
Filio Dei, homo purus pro Deo vero.[10] Quomodo non tuam
affectuosissimam animam pertransiret haec auditio,[11] quando et
nostra, licet saxea, licet ferrea pectora, sola recordatio scindit?[12]

Non mirermini, fratres, quod Maria Martyr in anima fuisse
dicatur.[13] Miretur qui non meminerit[14] se audivisse Paulum inter
maxima Gentium crimina memorantem quod sine affectione

---

7   vis, vim, vi, pl. vires, f., *force, power, strength: the force of sorrow.* Non
     immerito praedicemus: *not unworthily do we proclaim her,* plusquam
     martyrem, *to be more than a martyr,* in qua affectus compassionis, *in
     whom the feeling of compassion,* excesserit—excedere (3) perfect
     subjunctive, *exceeded,* sensum corporeae passionis, *of bodily passion.*

8   Bernard suggests that the real sword that pierced Mary's heart was
     that speech, sermo, sermonis, of Jesus on the cross, Mulier, ecce
     filius tuus: *Woman, behold thy son.* An, introducing a question, non
     tibi plusquam gladius fuit sermo ille: *was not that remark more of a
     sword to you,* revera pertransiens animam, *truly penetrating the soul,*
     et pertingens usque ad divisionem animae et spiritu, *and attaining
     even to the division of soul and spirit.*

9   *What a change!*

10   Bernard imagines Mary's reaction to he son's words: servus pro
     domino, *the servant for the master,* discipulus pro Magistro, *the pupil
     for the teacher, the son of Zebedee for the son of God, a pure man—purely
     a man—for true God.*

11   Quomodo non, *how not,* pertransiret, *how would it not pierce* tuam
     affectuossimam animam, *your most loving soul,* haec auditio, *this
     listening,* literally, perhaps: *hearing this: how could not hearing this
     transfix your most loving soul . . .*

12   Now the contrast: quando, *when,* et nostra, understand, anima, *our
     soul too,* licet saxea, *although stony,* licet ferrea pectora, *although our
     breasts are iron,* sola recordatio scindit, *the recalling alone sunders.*

13   Miremini is the imperfect subjunctive of the deponent miror, *you
     should not wonder,* quod Maria Martyr in anima fuisse dicatur: *the
     infinitive is past,* fuisse, *that Mary is said to have been a martyr in her
     soul.*

14   *Let him wonder who does not remember himself having heard Paul,*
     memorantem, *recalling,* inter maxima crimina Gentium, *among the
     greatest crimes of the Gentiles,* quod sine affectione fuissent: *that they
     were without affection.*

fuissent. Longe id fuit a Mariae visceribus, longe sit a servulis ejus.[15] Sed forte quis dicat: Numquid non eum praescierat mor iturum?[16] Et indubitanter. Numquid non sperabat continuo[17] resurrecturum? Et fideliter. Super haec doluit crucifixum?[18] Et vehementer. Alioquin quisnam[19] tu, frater, aut inde tibi haec sapientia, ut mireris plus Mariam compatientem quam Mariae Filium patientem? Ille etiam mori corpore potuit; ista commori corde non potuit?[20] Fecit illud caritas, qua majorem nemo habuit; fecit et hoc caritas, cui post illam similis altera non fuit.

---

15 Longe fuit...longe sit: *this was far from the case with the heart—insides, viscera—of Mary; may it be far from her servants.*

16 The future infinitive from **morior; numquid,** introducing a question expecting a negative answer. **Praescierat** from **praescire** (3): *did he not foresee that he would die?* **Indubitanter!** *Without any doubt.*

17 **Continuo,** adverb: *at once, immediately:* As in the previous question, the verbs are imperfect and future infinitive, respectively.

18 **Dolet** from **dolere** (2), *to suffer pain, to grieve:* its object is **crucifixum.**

19 **Quisnam,** *what then,* **alioquin:** the suggestion seems to be: *how then, brother, can you think otherwise;* or *whence come this wisdom to you:* **ut mireris,** *that you should wonder,* **plus,** *more about* **Mariam compatientem,** *Mary suffering along with,* **quam Filium Mariae patientem,** *than the suffering son of Mary.*

20 **Ille ... illa:** *he ... she; the son* **potuit,** the perfect of **possum, posse, potui,** *to be able,* **mori,** the infinitive, **corpore,** *in body: He could die in the body; could she not co-die in her heart?*

Lesson Eighteen
Homilia Sancti Gregorii Papae

In illo tempore: Ingressus Jesus perambulabat Jericho.[1] *Et ecce vir, nomine Zachaeus, et hic princeps erat publicanorum, et ipse dives. Et reliqua.*

Homilia sancti Gregorii
(Lib. 27 Moral., cap. 27, post medium)

Si veraciter sapientes esse atque ipsam sapientiam contemplari appetimus, stultos nos humiliter cognoscamus.[2] Relinquamus noxiam sapientiam, discamus laudabilem fatuitatem.[3] Hinc quippe scriptum est: Stulta mundi elegit Deus, ut confundat sapientes. Hinc rursum dicitur:[4] Si quis videtur inter vos sapiens esse in hoc saeculo, stultus fiat,[5] ut sit sapiens. Hinc evangelicae historiae verba testantur quia Zachaeus, cum videre prae turba nihil posset, sycomori arborem ascendit, ut transeuntem Dominum cerneret.[6] Sycomorus quippe ficus fatua dicitur.

---

1   **Ingressus** is the past participle of the deponent **ingredior, ingredi, ingressus sum,** *to enter, go in,* and modifies Jesus; **perambulabat** is the imperfect of **perambulare** (1). **Princeps, -is** (3) *a chief, a leader,* **et ipse dives,** *and he was rich.*

2   **Veraciter** is an adverb, *truly;* the verb **appetimus,** from **appetere,** (3) although following **si,** is in the indicative. It governs indirect discourse, a clause with a subject in the accusative and a verb in the infinitive: here **nos** understood, *if we wish ourselves to be wiser,* **sapientes esse** and **ipsam sapientiam contemplari,** *and to contemplate wisdom itself.* **Contemplor** (1) is a deponent.

3   **Relinquamus** is the subjunctive of **relinquere** (3); **noxius, -a,-um,** *harmful;* **discere** (3), providing another subjunctive, **discamus.** **Fatuitas, -tatis,** *foolishness;* **laudabilis,** an adjective, *praiseworthy.*

4   **Quippe,** conjunction, *indeed, certainly;* **hinc,** adverb, *from here, hence.* **Stulta,** accusative, is the object of **elegit,** perfect of **eligere** (3); **mundus, -i,** m., *world.*

5   **Stultus fiat,** *let him become foolish,* **ut sit sapiens,** *that he might be wise.*

6   **Evangelicae historiae verba,** *the words of the Gospel story;* **prae turba,** *on account the crowds;* **transeuntem,** present participle, accusative singular, **transire** (3), *to pass by,* modifying **Dominum. Ficus fatua,** *a*

Pusillus itaque Zachaeus sycomorum subiit et Dominum vidit:[7] quia, qui mundi stultitiam humiliter eligunt, ipsi Dei sapientiam subtiliter contemplantur. Pusillitatem namque nostram ad videndum Dominum turba praepedit;[8] quia infirmitatem humanae mentis, ne lucem veritatis intendat, curarum saecularium tumultus premit. Sed prudenter sycomorum ascendimus, si provide[9] eam quae divinitus[10] praecipitur stultiam mente tenemus. Quid enim in hoc mundo stultius[11] quam amissa non quaerer, possessa rapientibus relaxare, nullam pro acceptis injuriis injuriam reddere, immo adjunctis aliis patientiam praebere.[12]

Quasi enim sycomorum nos ascendere Dominus praecepit, cum dicit: Qui aufert quae tua sunt, ne repetas; et rursum: Si quis te percusserit in dexteram maxillam, praebe illi et alteram.[13] Per sycomorum Dominus transiens cernitur: quia per hanc sapientem stultiam, etsi necdum, ut est, solide, jam tamen per contemplationis lumen Dei sapientia quasi in transitu videtur, quam videre nequeunt qui sibi sapientes esse videntur; quia, ad con-

---

foolish fig tree: the noun is feminine, as you can tell from the adjective.

7   **Pusillus, -a, -um,** *little,* modifying Zachaeus; **subere** (3), here, *to climb: Therefore, the diminuitive Zachaeus climbed a sycamore and saw the Lord: beause, those who humbly choose the foolishness of the world, minutely contemplate the wisdom of God.*

8   **Praepedire** (3), *to entangle the feet, shackle, fetter;* **pusillitas, -atis.** f. **Ad videndum Deum:** gerundive of **videre** (3): *for seeing God. The crowd hinders our littleness from seeing God.* **Tumultus curarum saecularium,** *the tumult of worldly cares;* **premere** (3), *presses on the infirmity of our mind,* **ne lucem veritatis intendat,** *lest it tend to the light of truth.*

9   Adverb = *with foresight.*

10   Adverb.

11   The comparative: *more stupid, more foolish.*

12   Gregory here lists the acts of the Christian which must seem folly to the worldly: **amissa non quaerere:** *not to seek what is lost;* **possessa rapientibus relaxare,** *to cede one's goods to thieves;* **nullam pro acceptis injuriis injuriam reddere**—*not to return any injury for injuries received;* **immo adjunctis aliis patientiam praebere:** *indeed to shows patience to others around us.*

13   Following Christ's admonitions is likened to climbing the sycamore with Zachaeus—a book about Thomas Merton is called *The Man in the Sycamore Tree*—**qui aufert quae tua sunt, ne repetas:** *he who takes away those things which are yours—don't ask for them back:* **ne repetas,** a subjunctive. *The sycamore is the means whereby we will see the Lord as he passes by.*

conspiciendum Dominum, in elata cogitationum suarum turba
deprehensi, adhuc sycomori arborem non invenerunt.[14]

---

14   This is a complicated construction; **quia per hanc stultitiam,** *for through this foolishness,* (to see) **sapientem,** *the wise one,* **etsi necdum, ut est, solide,** *although not yet as he is, that is, firmly,* **jam tamen,** *yet now,* **per lumen contemplationis Dei,** *through the light of the contemplation of God,* **sapientia quasi in transitu,** *wisdom as it were in transit is seen,* **quam,** *which,* **qui sibi sapientes esse videntur,** *those who seem to themselves wise,* **nequeant videre,** *are unable to see.* Why? **Quia ad conspiciendum Dominum,** *because in order to see the Lord,* **deprehensi elata turba cogitationum suaram,** *they are in the grips of the stirred up crowd of their own thoughts, and have not yet found the sycamore tree.*

Saint John Chrysostom
Homilia 36 in Ioannem

In illo tempore: Erat dies festus Judaeorum et ascendit Jesus Jerosoly-mam. Et reliqua.

Quis hic curationis modus?[1] quale mysterium subindicatur?[2] Neque enim sine causa haec scripta sunt;[3] sed futura nobis quasi in figuribus et imagine describit, ne,[4] si res stupenda accideret inexspectata, auditorum multorum fidem aliquatenus labefac-taret.[5] Quaenam igitur haec descriptio?[6] Futurum baptisma dan-dum erat, plenum virtute et gratia maxima, baptisma quod peccata omnia ablueret, quod ex mortuis vivos redderet.[7] Haec

---

1   Quis agrees with **modus; hic** is the masculine deomonstrative—hic, haec, hoc—and **curatio, -onis,** f. means *a taking care, attention, man-agement. What kind of curing is this? What mystery is signified?*

2   Qualis, qualis, quale, *what kind:* subindicare (1) *intimate, indicate.*

3   *Everything in Scripture is for our instruction;* a truth expressed nega-tively here: **haec** is nominative plural, neuter, the subject of the perfect passive of **scribere** (2); **sine** = *without, sans.* **sed** contrasts with the opening **neque.**

4   **Ne,** *lest,* will introduce a subjunctive, and so will the **si** of the dependent clause; the latter governs **accideret—accidere** (3), *come about, occur*—whose subject is **res,** modified first by **inexspectata**—past participle of **inexspectare** (1)—and **stupenda,** a gerundive from **stupere** (2), a verbal adjective in the passive voice, *to be stunned by.*

5   This is the subjunctive governed by **ne;** it is from **labefactare** (1), *to make totter, shake, loosen;* **aliquatenus** is an adverb meaning *to a certain degree, in some measure.* **Auditorum multorum,** one is tempted to call this a genitive absolute, à la Greek: *lest many things being heard, (they) should to some degree shake faith.*

6   **Descriptio, -onis,** f., *a representation by writing of signs.* **Quaenam** = *what then?*

7   A lengthy answer to the question just put. Notice that **baptisma** is neuter, which explains both **futurum** and the **dandum** in the gerun-dive from **dare. Plenum** takes two ablatives, *full of virtue and the greatest grace.* **Ablueret** is from **abluere** (3) and **redderet** from **red-dere** (3), both subjunctive imperfect, the object of the first **omnia**

ergo ut in imagine depinguntur in piscina et in aliis multis.[8] Et
primo quidem aquam dedit, quae corporum maculas[9] ablueret,
sordesque non veras, sed tales existimatas,[10] ex funere nempe, ex
lepra, et similes; multaque videre est eadem de causa[11] in veteri
lege per aquam mundata.[12]

Sed ad propositum jam redeamus.[13] Primo itaque, ut diximus,
corporum maculas, deinde varias infirmitates per aquam solvi[14]
curat. Ut enim nos Deus ad baptisimi gratiam propius re-
duceret,[15] non jam maculas solum, sed et morbos[16] sanat. Imagines enim quae propius ad veritatem accedunt, et in baptismate,
et in passione, et in aliis magis conspicuae sunt quam
vetustiores.[17] Quemadmodum enim qui prope regem sunt satel-
lites, remotioribus sunt honorationes; ita et in figuris factum
est.[18] Et Angelus descendens turbabat aquam,[19] et sanandi vim

---

peccata—*that this baptism might wash away all sins; and might restore
the living from the dead.*

8   **Haec** is neuter plural, the subject of **depinguntur**, from **depingo,
depingere, depinxi, depinctus**, *depict, portray,* a third person plural
present passive. **Piscina, -ae**, f. literally a tank for fish—**piscis, -is,**
m.—but here, *pool*.

9   **macula, -ae**, f., *blemish, stain.* Repetition of **ablueret**.

10   **Sordesque—sordes, -is**, f., *dirt, filth*—which like the **maculae** are not
truly such but thought to be—**exsistimare** (1); and St. John Chrysostom goes on to list what he means: *leprosy,* **ex funere**, from **funus,
-eris**, n., *burial*, **et similes**, *and like or similar things.*

11   **Eadem de causa**—Latin often brackets a preposition with an adjective and its noun.

12   **Mundata**—from **mundare** (1), *to clean*—**sunt** being understood, this
is a perfect passive, whose subject is **multa**.

13   **Redeamus**—subjunctive, *let us return,* **ad propositum**, *to the topic
proposed*.

14   The passive infinitive from **solvere** (3).

15   The subjunctive required by **ut**, *in order that.*

16   **Morbus, -i**, m., *disease, sickness;* **curare** (1), *to heal, cure.*

17   **Vetustiores** is contrasted with **conspicuae** as modifying the images
which more properly indicate the truth to be revealed, whether in
baptism, the passion, or other things. **Vetustus, -a, -um**, means *old,*
but here perhaps *antiquated, old-fashioned,* and in the comparative,
more antiquated, as opposed to **conspicuus, -a, -um**, *visible.* One might
think that it is the fresh image as opposed to the stale whose fit-
tingness St. John Chrysostom is noting.

18   We are now given a figure to explain what has been said of figures:
quemadmodum, *just as, those close to the king are furthest from being
honored:* that is, images which may seem closer to what is imaged can

indebat ipsi,[20] ut discerent Judaei,[21] Angelorum Dominum multo magis posse animae morbos omnes curare.[22] Sed, quemadmodum hic aquarum natura non simpliciter curabat (alioquin enim semper id faceret),[23] sed Angeli operatione id fiebat;[24] sic in nobis non aqua simpliciter[25] operatur, sed, postquam Spiritus gratiam acceperit,[26] tunc omnia solvit peccata.

Circa hanc piscinam jacebat multitudo magna infirmorum, caecorum, claudorum, aridorum, aquae motum exspectantium.[27] Sed tunc infirmitas impedimento erat quominus is qui vellet, sanaretur;[28] nunc autem unusquisue potestatem accedendi habet.[29] Non enim Angelus est qui aquam movet, sed Angelorum Dominus omnia efficit.[30] Nec dicere possumus: Dum ego accedo,

---

distract us from it to themselves, perhaps; whereas simple things like water will not.

19 **Angelus descendens**—modified by the present participle of **descendere** (3)—*descending, disturbs,* **turbare** (1), **aquam,** from **aqua, aquae,** f.

20 **Indebat** has as its object **vim sanandi**—the power of healing, the gerundive from **sanare**—**ipsi,** to it, following the prefix of the compound verb, **in + dare.**

21 **Ut,** *in order that,* **discerent,** subjunctive from **disco, discere, didici, doctus** (3), **Iudaei,** *the Jews. In order that the Jews might learn . . .*

22 **Multo magis,** adverbial phrase, *much more,* **posse curare,** *can cure,* **morbos animae,** *diseases of the soul.* The genitives **Angelorum Dominum** serve as subject, where in a normal Latin construction we would expect accusatives: "learn that angels of the Lord can." The text of course has its origin in the Greek.

23 *If it were a natural property of water to cure, it would always do so.*

24 *But this came about,* **fiebat,** *by the operation of the angel*—it was miraculous.

25 **Simpliciter,** as such, *simply as water.*

26 This is the perfect subjunctive of **accipere** (3).

27 Modifying **infirmorum,** the genitive plural of the present participle of **exspectare** (1). And the nature of these ills is specified: **magna multitudo infirmorum, caecorum, claudorum aridorum**—*the blind, the crippled, the shriveled.*

28 A contrast: **tunc,** *then,* **infirmitas impedimento erat,** *illness was as an impediment,* **quominus** = *that not, lest,* **is qui vellet,** *he who might wish,* **sanaretur,** *might be cured,*

29 **Nunc autem,** *now however,* **unusquisque,** *anyone,* **potestatem habet,** *has the power,* **accedendi,** *of approaching.* The gerundive from **accedere** (3).

30 A precision: *it is not the angel, but the Lord of angels, who does everything.*

alius ante me descendit.[31] Sed, si totus orbis venerit, gratia non consumitur,[32] neque vis vel operatio deficit,[33] sed semper eadem manet. Ac, quemadmodum solares radii quotidie illuminant,[34] nec absumuntur, neque quod multis subministrentur, lucis quispiam amittunt;[35] sic, immo multo minus, Spiritus operatio minuitur[36] a multitudine accipientium. Hoc autem factum est ut qui discerent[37] in aqua curandos esse corporis morbos, et hac in re diu exercitati essent, facilius crederent[38] etiam morbos animi posse curari.[39]

---

31 A beautiful contrast. *Nor can we say, when I wished to descend, someone got there before me. The whole world can precede me, and I am not prevented.*

32 **Consumere (3),** *to use up,* so **gratia non consumitur,** *grace is not used up.*

33 **Deficere (3),** *fail, fade:* the **vis** and **operatio,** *the power and action* **gratiae** *does not fail.* **Manet** from **manere (2).**

34 **Quemadmodum,** another simile: *the rays of the sun,* **radii solares,** *which daily,* **quotidie,** *shine,* **illuminant** from **illuminare (1). Absumo, absumere, absumpsi, absumptus,** *to lessen, destroy, consume.*

35 **Subministrare (1),** *to aid, give, furnish, supply;* **amittere (3),** *take away.* **Quispiam,** *any, anything,* **lucis,** *of light.*

36 **Minuo, minere, minui, minutus,** *to make smaller, diminish.* **Immo multo minus,** *indeed much less;* **operatio Spiritus,** this is the subject of **minuitur.**

37 **Ut qui discerent,** *in order that anyone might learn*

38 **Facilius crederent:** *they might more easily believe.* **Diu,** adverb, *for a long time.*

39 Here is the whole point of the pool: *that from it we might learn, from the long experience of it, that if the ills of the body can be cured, so can the ills of the soul.*

Canticle of Hezechiah

1. Ego dixi: In dimidio dierum meorum vadam ad portas inferi frustratus residuo annorum meorum.
2. Dixi: Non jam videbo Dominum in terra viventium non jam conspiciam hominem inter habitatores terrae.
3. Habitatio mea dissolvetur, et auferetur ab me ut tentorium pastorum.
4. Convolvo sicut textor vitam meam; a filo mea abscindit die nocteque crucias me.
5. Vociferor usque ad mane; sicut leo confingit omnia ossa mea die nocteque crucias me.
6. Ut hirundo, sic pipio, gemo ut columba.
7. Deficiunt oculi mei suspicientes in altum, Domine, vim patior, adesto mihi.
8. Quid loquar? Nam ipse dixit mihi et ipse fecit! complebo omnes annos meos, superata amaritudine animae meae.
9. Quos tuetur Dominus, illi vivunt, et inter eos complebitur vita spiritus mei: sanum me fecisiti et servasti vivum!
10. Ecce, in salutem mutavit amaritudinem meam: tu enim servasti animam meam a fovea interitus; nam post te projecisti omnia peccata mea.
11. Profecto non infernus celebrat te, neque mors te laudat; non sperant, qui descendunt in foveam, fidelitatem tuam.
12. Vivens, vivens, celebrat te, et ego hodie: pater filiis notam facit fidelitatem tuam.
13. Dominus servat me: ideo psalmos meos cantabimus omnibus diebus vitae nostrae in domo Domini.

Let's plunge right in. You are going to be pleasantly surprised by how within your reach this passage is.

1. Ego dixi: In dimidio dierum meorum vadam ad portas inferi frustratus residuo annorum meorum.

No problem with the opening words: the first person singular of the perfect tense of **dicere,** a verb of the third conjugation. And you know what **ego** means: the first person pronoun. **Vadam** is the first person singular future of the third conjugation verb, **vado:** *I will go.* Where? **ad portas inferi.** The noun is accusative plural first declension after **ad,** and **inferi** is genitive singular. When? **In dimidio dierum meorum.** Although the influence goes in the opposite direction, one is reminded of the opening of the **Inferno,** *Nel mezzo del cammin di nostra vita,* a line Dorothy Sayer translated thus, "Midway this way of life we're bound upon." *In the midst of my days. In the noon of my life, I will go unto the gates of hell.* **Frustratus** modifies **ego;** it comes from **frustrare,** first conjugation, and is the past participle = *cheated,* **residuo**—an ablative—as to the rest **annorum meorum,** *of my years.* **Annus** is a noun of the second declension.

2. **Dixi: Non jam videbo Dominum in terra viventium**
   non jam conspiciam hominem inter habitatores terrae.

Non jam = *not now, no longer;* **videbo** of course is the first person singular future of **videre.** *I will no longer see the Lord.* Where? **In terra viventium**—*in the land of the living.* **Viventium** is the genitive plural of the present participle of **vivere,** namely, **vivens,** plural **viventes,** genitive plural, **viventium. Conspiciam** is another first person singular future, of **conspicere** (3) = *behold, descry. I will no longer behold* **hominem,** the accusative of **homo, hominis, homini, hominem, homine,** meaning of course *man.* Where will the speaker no longer see man? **Inter habitatores terrae. Inter** means *among* and **habitatores** is the accusative plural of **habitor** = *inhabitant.*

3. **Habitatio mea dissolvetur, et auferetur ab me ut**
   tentorium pastorum

No problem with the noun or its modifier. **Dissolvetur** is the third person singular passive present—*is dissolved, broken up.* **Auferetur** is another passive, of the compound formed of **ab** and **fero, ferre, tuli, latus, abferre,** or **auferre. Auferetur** = *is carried off.* What? Still **habitatio mea.** How? **Ut tentorium pastorum. Ut** here means *as* (**sicut** = *just as*), **tentorium** is a neuter noun meaning what its first syllable means in English, **pastorum** is the genitive plural of **pastor,** *shepherd.*

4. **Convolvo sicut textor vitam meam; a filo mea abscindit**
   die nocteque crucias me.

Convolvo is first person singular present tense = *I roll up*. What? **Vitam meam.** How? **Sicut textor. Textor, textoris** means *weaver.* **Abscindit** is third person singular of **abscindere.** *He cuts me* **a filo,** *from the thread.* Classically, this would suggest the thread of life. *I roll up my life like a weaver; he cuts me from the thread (the loom).* **Die nocteque crucias.** This will close the next verse as well. **Die** and **nocte** are ablatives, of **dies** and **nox, noctis,** respectfully. **-que** means *and.* **Crucias** is second person singular of **cruciare** *to torment.* The verse thus moves from first to third to second person in its verbs.[1]

5. **Vociferor usque ad mane; sicut leo confingit omnia ossa mea die nocteque crucias me.**

Vociferor is first person singular, the form is passive, but the verb is deponent, so it means, *I cry out,* **usque ad mane,** *even unto* **mane,** an indeclinable noun meaning *morning.* **Sicut leo,** *like a lion,* **confringit,** *he breaks* **ossa mea,** *my bones.* And then the reiteration of: *You torture me day and night.*

6. **Ut hirundo, sic pipio, gemo ut columba.**

Hirundo is nominative singular (its genitive is **hirundinis**) and the initial **ut** means *as,* not *in order that: like a swallow, so do I peep;* **ut columba,** *like a dove,* **gemo,** *I moan. I twitter like a swallow and mourn like a dove.*

7. **Deficiunt oculi mei suscipientes in altum, Domine, vim patior, adesto mihi.**

Oculi, modified by **mei,** is the subject of **deficiunt,** the third person plural present tense of **deficere** = *to fail. My eyes fail.* When? **Suspicientes in altum.** This is the nominative plural of the present participle of **aspicere: aspiciens** in the nominative singular, **suspicientes** in the plural. This modifies **oculi.** *My eyes, looking on high, fail.* **Domine, vim patior.** The Lord is addressed in the vocative case. **Patior** is first person singular, passive in form, but a deponent verb, therefore having an active meaning. **Patior, pati, passum sum. Vim** is the accusative singular of **vis,** *power* or *force. Lord, I feel your strength, suffer it.* **Adesto mihi. Adesto** is from the compound verb formed of **ad** and **esse.** When you answer roll call in Latin

---

1   The new Vulgate has "**praecisa est velut a texente vita mea**" = *my life is cut off as by a weaver.*

class, you say **adsum,** *I am present.* **Esto** is the singular imperative
of **esse.** Thus: *be near me, be present to me.*

    8. **Quid loquar? Nam ipse dixit mihi et ipse fecit!**
       complebo omnes annos meos,
       superata amaritudine animae meae.

    Quid loquar? *What may I say?* **Loquar** is the subjunctive of the
deponent verb **loquor. Nam** means *for,* **dixit mihi** is now obvious
to you, **et ipse fecit!** *For he told me and he did it.* In the sense of: *He
promised and he kept his word.* **Complebo omnes annos meos.** The
verb is first person singular future tense or **complere,** *to complete.*
Superata amaritudine—an ablative absolute. **Amaritudo** has as its
ablative singular **amaritudine** and **superata** is the past participle
of the first conjugation verb **supero** in the ablative singular
feminine to agree with the noun. *My bitterness being overcome* or
better *the bitterness of my soul being overcome.*

    9. **Quos tuetur Dominus, illi vivunt,**
       et inter eos complebitur vita spiritus mei:
       sanum me fecisti et servasti vivum!

    Quos—accusative plural masculine of the relative pronoun =
whom. Why accusative? The object of **tuetur.** But isn't that passive?
Yes, but you guessed it, another deponent verb, **tueor, tueri, tuitus.**
Its subject is the Lord. Whom the Lord regards, **illi vivunt.** You
remember that **illi** is the nominative plural of **ille** and the plural
has the sense of *they;* **vivunt** is a nice straightforward third person
plural present tense of the third conjugation verb **vivere. Et inter
eos** = *and among them,* **vita,** *the life,* **spiritus mei,** *of my spirit,*
complebitur, a third person singular future passive of **complere.**
Among them the life of my spirit will be completed or fulfilled. **Sanum** is
an accusative singular modifying **me,** which is the object of the
third person singular perfect tense **fecisti** = *you have made me well,*
et servasti vivum, *and kept or preserved (me) alive.*

    10. **Ecce, in saltutem mutavit amaritudinem meam;**
       tu enim servasti animam meam a fovea interitus;
       nam post te projecisti omnia peccata mea.

    Ecce, *behold, see!* **Mutavit** is the third person singular perfect
tense of the first conjugation verb **mutare,** *to change.* He changed
what? **Amaritudinem meam,** *for me,* **mihi, in salutem,** *into*

salvation: Behold, for me he changed my bitterness into salvation. **Tu,** now addressing the Lord, **enim,** *for You preserved my soul* **a fovea interitus. Fovea** is a first declension noun, here in the ablative singular after **a:** *from the pit of destruction.* **Interitus** is a noun of the fourth declension, and this is its genitive singular. It means destruction. **Projecisti**—from **projicere, projeci, projectus,** from which our *project* comes. Here the second person singular of the perfect tense along with **post te** means *you have put behind you* **omnia peccata mea.**

11. Profecto non infernus celebrat te, neque mors te laudat;
non sperant, qui descendunt in foveam, fidelitatem tuam.

Profecto is an adverb meaning *indeed* or *truly.* **Celebrat** is the verb, third person singular present tense first conjugation. Its subject is **infernus.** Yes, *hell, or the underworld, the place of the dead.* **Neque** = *neither, nor;* **mors** of course is *death,* and **laudat** is parsed just like **celebrat:** *Truly, the underworld does not celebrate you nor death praise you.* **Non sperant.** The verb is first conjugation, **sperare,** so you know this is third person plural. What is its subject? **Qui descendant in foveam:** *they who go down into the pit.* What is its object? **Fidelitatem tuam.** So: *they who go down into the pit do not hope in your trustworthiness.*

12. Vivens, vivens, celebrat te, et ego hodie:
pater filiis notam facit fidelitatem tuam.

The thought is continued, emphatically, with the repetition of **vivens.** *It is the living, the living (who)* **celebrat te,** *celebrate you;* **ut ego hodie,** *as I (do) today.* **Pater** is the subject of **facit** whose object is **fidelitatem tuam** modified by **notam.** *The father makes your fidelity known.* To whom? **Filiis.** *To (his) sons.*

13. Dominus servat me: ideo psalmos meos cantabimus
omnibus diebus vitae nostrae in domo Domini.

Dominus servat me. This gives you no difficulty whatsoever. *The Lord preserves me.* Therefore, **ideo, cantabimus** = first person plural future of **cantare:** *Therefore we shall sing my psalms.* How long? **Omnibus diebus vitae nostrae**—ablative of duration, **omnibus** modifying **diebus,** *for all the days,* **vitae nostrae,** *of our life.* Where? **In domo Domini.** *In the house of the Lord.*

Thomas Aquinas on the Canticle

One finds in Volume XXVIII of the edition of the works of St. Thomas Aquinas commissioned by Pope Leo XIII a gloss on the passage from Isaiah we know as the Canticle of Hezechiah. Thomas made this commentary while he was still a student—it is called a cursive commentary. It sticks very close to the text, and as we shall see Thomas in very concerned to discover the order and structure of what he comments on. The text that Thomas is commenting on differs somewhat from that which heads this chapter. I have introduced our numbering into Thomas's analysis of the canticle but, as you can seen, there is not always a perfect match of language. Nonetheless, translating Thomas is both good practice in Latin and an introduction to his biblical commentaries, though as mentioned this work on Isaiah is both early and merely a cursive reading of the text. Thomas's analysis provides an outline of the canticle, and you may want to make it even more more explicit by writing it out.

Ego dixi,[2] in quo tria facit: primo plangit[3] periculum quod evasit,[4] [1] secundo commemorat beneficium quo percepit:[5] *Domine, si sic, etc,* [9] tertio petit complementum[6] quod Deus promisit: *Domine salvum,* etc. [13] Plangit autem tria. Primo mortis horrorem: *In dimidio,* [1] id est in iuventute[7] mea, *ad*

---

2   This functions as the title of the canticle; Thomas then goes on to divide it into three parts. The first running from [1] through [8], the second from [9] through [12], and the third found in [13]. In the first part, according to Thomas, Hezechiah laments the troubles he has undergone; in the second he is mindful of the help he has received; in the third he asks the fulfillment of the promise.

3   Third person singular present of third conjugation verb **plango, plangere, planxi, planctus,** literally, *to beat,* but it came to mean *lament, mourn.* Hence the English adjective *plangent.*

4   Third person singular of the perfect tense of the third conjugation verb **evadere. Evasit** here means *he escaped.*

5   Third person singular of perfect tense of third conjugation verb **percipere.** *To perceive.*

6   **complementum,** a neuter noun meaning that which completes or fulfills.

7   **juventus, juventutis,** feminine noun meaning youth or, as some dictionaries make precise, the period between the twentieth and fortieth year, a rather commodious expanse.

portas inferi, id est limbum,[8] vel mortem vel sepulcrum,[9] (Eccli. ult.) "Vitam meam appropinquans," etc. Secundo plangit bonorum amissionem[10] quantum ad Dei visionem: *Quaesivi,* a Domino, quod suppleret[11] *residuum* mihi ablatum,[12] vel inquisivi apud me quantum[13] restaret mihi de vita. *Dixi* apud[14] me: *Non videbo,* [2] per speciem modo adhuc,[15] *in terra viventium,* in coelesti beatitudine, Ps. "Credo videre," etc.; vel Non videbo ulterius,[16] videndo templum et cultum eius, in terra viventium, scilicet Iudeorum, Mt. 22, "Non est Deus mortuorum," etc. Etiam quantum ad hominum societatem: *Non aspiciam hominem* in hac vita viventem, Ier. xlix "Non habitabit ibi vir," etc.; vel *hominem,* Christum nobis promissum.[17] Etiam quantum ad filiorum posteritatem: *Generatio,* [3] scilicet filiorum, quia nondum[18] filios

---

8   This means *limbo,* and it is in the accusative, governed by **ad.** It is a neuter noun.

9   *Place of burial:* **sepulchrum, sepuchri,** neuter noun. Like **limbum** and **mortem** it is governed by **ad** in **ad portas inferi,** since these are interpretations of the gates of hell.

10   Meaning *loss;* it is in the accusative as the object of **plangit,** and takes the genitive plural, **bonorum:** *he laments the loss of goods.* **Quantum ad** is a locution meaning *with respect to: and he will lament the loss of good, with respect to the vision of God, or with respect to what remaining life was meant for him,* and then in [2] with respect to the society of men, and in [3] with respect to children, his posterity. And in [4] he laments the brevity of life. Of course the major division of the lamentation turns on [1] the horror of death, [2] the loss of goods, subdivided as we have seen, and [4] anxiety of heart.

11   A subjunctive of the second conjugation verb **suppleo, supplere, supplevi, suppletus** = *to fill up, make full, complete, supply.*

12   Of what verb is this the past participle? It modifies **residuum.**

13   This **quantum** means *how much.*

14   This preposition makes sense in Latin and perhaps in English, if we would translate it as *with me.* But we wouldn't say, "I sought with me how much life might remain to me." Better: *I sought within myself* = *I asked myself.* **Apud** takes the accusative = *at, near, by, with.*

15   A Pauline reference: **modo** = *now,* **adhuc** = *still,* **per speciem** = *through a glass;* in the land of the living is interpreted as *heavenly beatitude.*

16   Adverb = *any longer, further: I will no longer see.* Thomas glosses this **videndo templum et cultum:** *by seeing the temple and its mode of worship,* taking, *in the land of the living,* to mean here, *in the land of the Jews.*

17   Thomas sees an allusion to Christ, *the one promised to us:* **nobis promissum.**

18   **Nondum** means *not yet.* Hezechiah laments that he will have no progeny—**filiorum posteritatem. Plicata** is the past participle of the

habebat, convoluta, plicata ne ad posteros extendatur, supra xxiiij "Auferetur quasi tabernaculum"[19] etc. Etiam quantum ad vitae brevitatem: [4] *precisa est velut a texente*, dum adhuc texit,[20] tela imperfecta; *ordirer* in iuventute, Iob vij "Dies mei velocius" etc.

Tertio plangit cordis anxietatem. Et primo quantum ad mortis continuam expectationem: [4] *De mane*, scilicet dicebam, *usque ad vesperam*[21] *finies me* morte, et tunc non moriens *sperabam* [5] iterum *usque ad mane*, ut simul cum morte dolor aegritudinis finiretur; nihilominus *quasi leo sic contrivit*, langor, vel ipse Deus per dolorem aegritudinis, Iob vij "Si dormiero," etc. Secundo quantum ad spei dilationem;[22] ubi ponit tria: sperantis compunctionem: [6] *Sicut pullus hirundinis* expectat matrem, quia non videt, *ut columba*, cum gemitu scilicet, Nam secundo "Gementes ut columbae" etc. Ponit etiam spei dilationem: [7] *Attenuati*, quasi fatigati,[23] *suspicientes* per spem, Prov. xiij "Spes quae differtur" etc., Ps. "Levavi oculos meos" etc. Ponit etiam quandam cum Deo disceptationem:[24] *Domine vim patior*, quasi: violentia fit mihi, ultra merita affligor; *responde*, id est fideiubeas pro me. [8] *Quid*

---

first conjugation verb **plicare**, meaning *to fold up, double up*; it modifies **generatio, -onis**, a feminine noun.

19   Another word for tent. **Quantum ad vitae brevitatem** = *with respect to the brevity of life*.

20   **Tela, telae**, feminine, *a web, what is woven*. It relates to the verb **texo, texere, texui, textus**, the third person singular of whose present tense occurs just before.

21   *Third, he laments anxiety of heart. And first with respect to the continuous expectation of death: From morning, namely I have said, unto evening you bind me with death, and then, not dying, I hoped again until morning, and along with death the sorrow of illness will be finished; nonetheless he(God or languor) crushed me like a lion . . . through the sorrow of illness . . .*

22   **Dilatio, dilationis**, feminine = *delay, deferral, putting off*. From **differe**. Second, with respect to the deferral of hope, where he makes three points. **Compunctionem sperantis:** *the compunction of the one hoping.* The noun comes from **compungere**, a third conjugation verb, meaning *to prick, needle, puncture*. This would provide an alternative metaphor to the gnawing of conscience.

23   *As it were, worn out or tired, looking up through or with hope. "I have lifted up my eyes,"* Psalm 120:1.

24   **Disceptatio, disceptationis**, a feminine noun meaning *debate, argument, dispute*. This leads to the various allusions to Job that follow. *Has violence been done him; has he been afflicted more than he deserves?* **Quid dicam?** *What am I saying;* as if turning on himself, Thomas notes. **Quid possem contra Deum proponere?** *What can I propose or urge against God?*

dicam?, quasi in se reversus: Quid possem contra Deum proponere? *Aut quid respondebit?*, quando debet ad interrogatoria
respondere, *cum ipse fecerit me*, vel poenam meam, Iob ix "Si
voluerit contendere cum eo" etc., infra xlv "Numquid contradicit
factori" etc. Tertio quantum ad praeteritorum recordationem:[25]
recogitabo annos in quibus bona passum sum, vel etiam in
quibus tibi peccavi, Iob vij "Loquar in tribulatione spiritus" etc.

[9] Domine si sic. Hic commemorat beneficium quod
suscepit;[26] et primo correctionem: *Si sic vivitur*, id est si tammesera
est vita hominum, vel si per tribulationes acquiritu vita, Prv. vj
"Via vitae increpatio disciplinae" et ponit: *Ecce in pace* [10] quasi:
popula (pacem) habente ab Assiriis, amaritudo mihi imminet,
Prov. xiiij "Risus dolori" etc. Secundo commemorat
liberationem, a poena: *tu autem eruisti animam*, vitam, et a culpa:
projecisti post tergum tuum vel meum, quasi obliviscens, *omnia
peccata mea*, Sap. xj "Misereris omnium Domine" etc.[27] Tertio
assignat liberationis rationem, et primo quantum ad mortis
inutilitatem: [11] *Quia non infernus*, id est damnati vel sepulti,
mors, diabolus vel mortui, *veritatem*, promissionum, vel filium,
Ps. "Non est in morte" etc.; secundo quantum ad vivorum
laudem: [12] *Vivens, vivens*, ad maiorem affirmationem, vel
propter duplicem vitam,[28] Ps. "Nos qui vivimus" etc.; tertio
quantum ad divinae laudis propagationem: *Pater filiis*, etc. Ps.
"Mandavit patribus nostris nota facere" etc. [13] Domine salvum.
Hic petit promissum expleri:[29] salvum me fac ab Assiriis, et a
langore, Ps. "Benedicam Dominum in omni tempore" etc.

---

25   *With respect to the recalling of past things: I will think back upon the years
in which I received good things, or even in which I sinned against you.*

26   *The benefit that he received.* **Suscipio, suscipere, suscepi, susceptus.**
His travails amount to a correction. ". . . *that is if the life of men is so
miserable, or if life is acquired through tribulations . . .*" and then Thomas
cites Proverbs 6:23. *"The path of life is a call to discipline. With respect to
[10] ". . . as if: while the people had peace with the Assyrians, bitterness was
imminent to me, Proverbs 14,13 "Laughter with sorrow, etc."*

27   Second he remembers his liberation from punishment: *you took away
my soul, life, and from guilt: you put behind the back, yours or mine, you
were one forgetting, all my sins . . .* Third he assigns the reason for the
liberation.

28   Thomas says the repetition may be for emphasis or to indicate the
two lives, this and the next, in which we praise God.

29   Hezechiah begs for the promise to be fulfilled. **Expleri** is a passive
infinitive. He wants relief from sorrow and from the Assyrians.

Lesson Twenty One
Saint Thomas Aquinas

THIS LESSON WILL CONTAIN TWO READINGS from Thomas, the first the preface he wrote to his commentary on a work called the *Liber de Causis*, The Book on the Causes. It is a difficult, Neoplatonic work, and the commentary itself is a taxing read. The preface, however, is pretty accessible. The second reading is Thomas's prologue to the third part of his masterpiece, the *Summa theologiae*.

Sancti Thomae de Aquino
super librum De Causis Exposiito

Sicut Philosophus dicit in X Ethicorum,[1] ultima felicitas hominis consistit in optima operatione quae est supremae potentiae, scilicet intellectus, respectu optimi intelligibilis.[2] Quia vero effectus per causam cognoscitur,[3] manifestum est quod causa secundum sui naturam est magis intelligibilis quam effectus,[4]

---

1   **Philosophus, -i,** m., like other medievals Thomas refers to Aristotle simply as the philosopher: **sicut dicit,** as Aristotle says, followed by a reference to the 10th book of the *Nicomachean Ethics,* chap. 7.

2   **Ultima,** a singular nominative feminine adjective, *ultimate,* modifying **felicitas, -tatis,** f., *felicity, happiness;* **hominis** is of course the genitive singular of **homo, -inis,** m., *man, a member of the human species;* **consistere** (3), a verb with a whole arsenal of meanings, the relevant one here being the English verb it suggests, *consists in;* **optima operatio:** another superlative to match **ultima:** the best operation or activity, which is that? **supremae potentiae,** the noun **potentia, -ae,** f., *power or capacity;* and what is man's highest capacity? **scilicet,** namely, **intellectus, -us,** *intellect.* Just any old act of intellect? **Respectu optimi intelligibilis: respectus, -us** is in the ablative here, *with respect to* or *of, the best or highest intelligible, the most intelleigible.* Ultimate human happiness = highest human activity, the intellect, bearing on the most intelligible thing. A suite of superlatives.

3   **Quia,** *because,* **vero,** *indeed, truly,* **effectus, -us,** *what is brought about, the effect,* **cognoscitur,** a third person singular passive of the present tense of **cognoscere** (3), *to know,* so: *is known;* **per causam,** *through the cause.* What is brought about is known through what brings it about: *the effect is known through the cause.* **Causa, -ae,** f.

4   **Manifestum est,** *it is manifest or evident,* **quod,** *that* (medieval Latin

etsi aliquando quoad nos effectus sint notiores causis propter hoc quod ex particularibus sub sensu cadentibus universalium et intelligibilium causarum cognitionem accipimus.[5]

Oportet igitur quod simpliciter loquendo primae rerum causae sint secundum se maxima et optima intelligibilia, eo quod sunt maxime entia et maxime vera cum sint aliis essentiae et veritatis causa, ut patet per Philosophum in II *Metaphysicae*,[6] quamvis huiusmodi primae causae sint minus et posterius notae quoad nos: habet enim se ad ea intellectus noster sicut oculus noctuae ad lucem solis quam propter excedentem claritatem perfecte percipere non potest.[7] Oportet igitur quod ultima felicitas

---

uses this construction unknown in classical Latin but akin to English); **causa secundum sui naturam,** *according to the nature of its,* **sui,** *its nature,* **magis intelligibilis quam effectus:** *is more intelligible than the effect.*

5   **Etsi,** *although,* **aliquando,** *sometimes,* **quoad nos,** *for us, with respect to us,* **effectus sint notiores causis:** the noun **effectus** is the nominative plural as its verb **sint** suggests: it is in the subjunctive; **notiores,** modifies **effectus,** and is the comparative of the adjective, **notus, -a, -um,** *known;* **notiores** = *more known,* **causis,** plural ablative, *than causes. Although sometimes for us effects are more known than (their) causes.* Why? **Propter hoc,** *on account of this, because,* **quod,** *that,* **accipimus,** first person plural present active of **accipere** (3), *take or receive: we receive,* **cognitionem,** the accusative singular of **cognitio, -onis, f.,** *knowledge,* **universalium et intelligibilium causarum,** three genitive plurals, two adjectives and one their noun, causes, **ex particularibus,** from particulars, ablative plural after **ex; sub sensu cadentibus:** that last word is the ablative plural of the present participle of **cadere** (3), *to fall, falling. Because we get knowledge of universal and intelligible causes from the particulars which fall under the sense.*

6   **Oportet,** *it is necessary,* a familiar impersonal verb in Thomas; **igitur,** *therefore,* **quod simpliciter loquendo:** this last is the gerundive from **loquor, loqui, locutus sum,** *to say, to speak,* simply *speaking,* that being the ablative of the gerundive; **primae rerum causae,** the noun here is in the plural and modified by **primae,** both nominatives, *the first causes,* **rerum,** a genitive plural of **res, rei, f.,** *thing,* so, *first causes of things,* **sint,** *are,* subjunctive, **secundum se,** *according to themselves, in themselves,* **maxima et optima intelligibilia,** two superlative modifiers of intelligible things, *the greatest and the best. So it is necessary absolutely speaking that the first causes of things be in themselves the most and best intelligible things.*

7   Why are the first causes the most intelligible things? **Eo quod,** *by this,* an ablative singular, *that* = *because,* **sunt maxime entia et maxima vera,** *they are the highest things and the most true;* why? **cum sint,** *since they are,* **causa essentiae et veritatis,** *the cause of the being and truth—* **essentia, -ae, f.,** the present participle of **esse; veritas, -tatis, f.** *truth—*

hominis quae in hac vita haberi potest, consistat in consideratione primarum causarum,[8] quia illud modicum quod de eis sciri
potest, est magis amabile et nobilius omnibus his quae de rebus
inferioribus cognosci possunt, ut patet per Philosophum in I De
partibus animalium;[9] secundum autem quod haec cognitio in
nobis perficitur post hanc vitam, homo perfecte beatus constituitur secundum illud Evangelii: "Haec est vita aeterna ut cognoscant te Deum verum unum." [Io. 17, 3][10]

---

aliis, *for other things,* dative plural of **alius, -a,-um.** *Since they are the
cause of the being and truth of other things.* **Ut patet,** this from **patere**
(2), *to be open, accessible,* **ut,** *as, as is evident,* **per Philosophum,** *through
Aristotle;* where? In *Metaphysics,* Bk. 2, 1. **Quamvis,** *although,* **primae
causae,** *first causes,* **huiusmodi,** *of this kind,* as is easily seen if we break
it into its components: **huius,** *of this,* **modus, -i,** m., *manner or kind;*
sunt minus et posterius notae quoad nos; *they are known less and later
by us.* And Thomas invokes one of Aristotle's powerful images.
Intellectus noster, *our intellect,* **habet enim se ad ea,** *has itself to them,*
is related to them: **se habere,** a reflexive, *is related to;* **sicut oculus
noctuae ad lucem solis: noctua, -ae,** f., *nightbird, owl, like the eye of an
owl to the light of the sun;* **quam,** *which,* the relative pronoun agreeing
with **lucem propter excedentem claritatem,** *on account of its exceed-
ing*—present participle from **excedere** (3)—*brightness,* **propter** calling for the accusative; **perfecte,** adverb, *perfectly,* **percipere non
potest:** *is unable to perceive perfectly.*

8   Despite their relative inaccessibility for us: **oportet igitur quod ultima felicitas hominis,** all this repeats language we have already
seen, *it is necessary that man's ultimate happiness,* **quae in hac vita
haberi potest,** the relative pronoun agrees with **felicitas,** and **haberi**
is a passive infinite: *which can be had,* **in hac vita,** *in this life,* the noun
and demonstrative adjective both ablative after the preposition **in;**
consistat in consideratione primarum causarum: *should consist,*
present subjunctive of consistere (3).

9   **Quia illud modicum,** *because that little bit,* **quod de eis sciri potest,**
which can be known of them—**sciri** is a passive infinitive of **scire** —**est
magis amabile:** *is more lovable,* the adjective agreeing with the neuter
noun **modicum, et nobilius,** the comparative of **nobilis,** *more noble,,*
omnibus his quae de rebus inferioribus cognosci possunt: the
comparative is followed by the ablative **omnibus,** modifying **his,**
more noble than all those things, that can be known, **cognosci,** another
passive infinitive, *of lesser things.* **Ut patet,** *as is evident from Aristotle
in The Parts of Animals, I, 5.*

10   Thomas now links the philosophical doctrine with the faith. **Secundum autem quod haec cognitio:** *however,* **autem,** *according as or
insofar,* **secundum quod,** *this knowledge,* **haec scientia,** *that is of the
first and most intelligible,* **perficitur in nobis,** *is perfected*—**perficere**
(3), third person singular passive, present—*in us,* **post hanc vitam,**
after this life; **homo perfecte beatus constituitur,** *a man is made perfectly
happy, according to that text of the Gospel,* **evangelium, -i,** n.: **Haec est**

Et inde est quod philosophorum intentio ad hoc principaliter erat[11] ut, per omnia quae in rebus considerabant, ad cognitionem primarum causarum pervenirent. Unde scientiam de primis causis ultimo ordinabant, cuius considerationi ultimum tempus suae vitae deputarent:[12] primo quidem incipientes a logica quae modum scientiarum tradit,[13] secundo procedentes ad mathematicam cuius etiam pueri possunt esse capaces,[14] tertio ad naturalem philosophiam quae propter experientiam tempore indiget,[15] quarto autem ad moralem philosophiam cuius iuvenis esse conveniens auditor non potest,[16] ultimo autem scientiae divinae insistebant quae considerat primas entium causas.[17]

---

vita aeterna: *this is life eternal*, ut cognoscant te, *that they might know*—a subjunctive of cognoscere (3)—Deum, in apposition to the accusative of the personal pronoun, te, verum unum: *true and one*, modifying Deum.

11 Et inde est quod: *and thence it is that*, intentio philosophorum, *the purpose or aim of philosophers*, erat, *was*, principaliter ad hoc, *chiefly for this*, ut pervenirent, *that they might come to, arrive at*—subjunctive from pervenire—ad cognitonem primarum causarum, *to knowledge of the first causes*. How? per omnia quae in rebus considerabant: *through or by means of all that they considered in things, in reality*.

12 *Since knowledge of first causes is gained through the study of everything else*, ultimo ordinabant, *they put last in order*, scientiam de primis causis; cuius considerationi: a genitive and a dative: *for the consideration of which*, deputarent, *they put off until*, or *set aside for*, ultimum tempus suae vitae: *the final phase of their life*.

13 Primo, an adverb, *first*, quidem, *indeed*, incipientes, present participle of incipere (3), *to begin*, nominative plural modifying the subject of deputarent; *indeed beginning first from or with logic*, quae modum scientiarum tradit: the verb is from tradere (3), the relative pronoun is feminine singular, because of logica, *which treats the mode of sciences*, that is, the manner of procedure that will lead to knowledge.

14 Secundo, adverb, *secondly*, procedentes ad mathematicam, *going on to mathematics*, the present participle, procedentes, is from procedere (3) ; cuius, *of which*, etiam pueri, *also boys, boys too, even children*, possunt esse capaces, *can be capable*, capax, -acis, *able to hold*.

15 Tertio, *third*, ad naturalem philosophiam, the noun philosophy and its modifier are in the accusative after ad, *to*, quae propter experientiam, *which*, natural philosophy, *because of experience*, tempore indiget—indigere (2), *to need: needs time because (of the need for) experience*.

16 Quarto autem ad moralem philosophiam, *fourth, on to moral philosophy*, cuius iuvenis esse conveniens auditor non potest: *of which, a youth can not be*, non potest esse, *a fitting student*, conveniens auditor. An Aristotelian point.

17 Ultimo, *finally*, the thing chiefly intended is taken up, scientiae divinae insistebant, the known and its adjective are governed by the

Tertia Pars Summae Theologiae, Prologus

Quia Salvator noster Dominus Iesus Christus, teste Angelo, populum suum salvum faciens a peccatis eorum (Mt. 1, 21),[18] viam veritatis nobis in seipso demonstravit, per quam ad beatitudinem immortalis vitae resurgendo pervenire possimus[19] necesse est ut, ad consummationem totius theologici negotii, post considerationem ultimi finis humanae vitae et virtutum ac vitiorum, de ipso omnium Salvatore ac beneficiis eius humano generi praestitis nostra consideratio subsequatur.[20]

Circa quam, primo considerandum occurrit de ipso Salvatore;[21]

---

in in the compound verb, *they entered upon divine science,* **quae considerat primas entium causas.** The new word here is the genitive plural or **ens, entis,** *a being.* So: *which considers the first causes of being.*

18   **Quia,** *because,* and then a very compound subject, **Salvator, -oris,** m., *one who saves, savior,* **noster,** *our,* **Dominus,** *Lord,* **Iesus Christus,** and then an ablative phrase, **teste angelo,** *the angel as witness,* **testis, -is,** as evident in the quotation from Matthew, "making his people safe from their sins," **demonstravit,** the perfect third person singular of **demonstrare** (1), *to show, point out,* **viam veritatis,** *the way of truth,* **nobis,** *for us,* **in seipso,** *in himself: Christ is the way and the truth.*

19   **Per quam,** *through which, by which,* the pronoun refers to **viam, possumus pervenire,** *we can arrive,* **ad beatitudinem immortalis vitae,** happiness here is in the accusative after **ad**—**beatitudo, -idinus,** f.—*to the happiness of immortal life,* **resurgendo,** *by rising again,* through resurrection; gerundive from **resurgere** (3).

20   This has implications for theological business: **necesse est ut,** *it is necessary that,* **ad consummationem totius theologici negotii: negotium, -i,** n. *business,* with **totius** and **theologici,** modifiying it: *for the completion of the theological enterprise as a whole, it is necessary that,* **post considerationem ultimi finis humanae vitae:** *after the consideration of the ultimate end of human life;* no problem there, linguistically; Thomas is referring to the Second Part of his *Summa;* **et virtutum ac vitium,** two genitive plurals, **ac = et:** *and of virtues and vices,* **ut subsequatur,** the subjunctive after **ut,** from the deponent verb **subsequor, subsequi, subsecutus sum,** *to follow on or after,* its subject is **nostra consideratio,** *it is necessary that our consideration go on to or about* **de ipso Salvatore,** *the Savior himself,* savior **omnium,** *of all,* **ac beneficiis eius praestitis,** *and his benefits presented,* **humano generi,** dative of **genus, generis,** n., *kin,* but more basically, *race: to the human race.*

21   **Circa quam,** this may be one of the two or three most frequent prepositions in Thomas: around literally, but rather, *about, concerning, which:* the accusative singular referring back to **consideratio;** the rest of the phrase is awkward, taken literally: *concerning which it occurs first that we ought to consider the Savior himself;* **occurrere** (3), has

secundo, de sacramentis eius, quibus salutem consequimur;[22]
tertio, de fine immortalis vitae, ad quem per ipsum resurgendo
pervenimus.[23]

Circa primum duplex consideratio occurit:[24] primo est de ipso
incarnationis mysterio, secundum quod Deus pro nostra salute
factus est homo; secunda de his quae per ipsum Salvatorem
nostrum, id est Deum incarnatum, sunt acta et passa.[25]

---

the verb *to run* at its base, and Thomas uses it impersonally:
considerandum is, of course, a gerundive.

22   **Secundo, de sacramentis eius;** Thomas is here giving us the main
subdivisions of the third part of his summary of theology;
sacramentum, -i, n., *sacrament,* here the ablative plural after **de; eius,**
his, that is, the Savior's; **quibus,** *by which, by means of which,* an
ablative, **consequimur,** first person plural, *we achieve or arrive at,*
salutem, accusative of **salus, -utis,** f., *health,* here: *salvation.*

23   **Tertio, de fine immortalis vitae: finis, -is,** m., *end, goal;* here in the
ablative singular after **de; vitae,** singular genitive of **vita, -ae,** f., *life,*
with the adjective **immortalis** agreeing with it; **ad quem,** *toward
which,* the relative pronoun agreeing in gender and number with
finis, per ipsum, *through him,* **resurgendo,** how? *by arising, through
resurrection,* **pervenimus:** *we arrive. Third, of immortal life, to which we
come through him by means of resurrection.*

24   Note the repetition of the phrase almost verbatim (that is a loan word
from the Latin, word for word); **Circa primum,** that is, *about the first
point* mentioned in the preceding paragraph, that the Savior himself
will be discussed first, **duplex,** *twofold, a dual* **consideratio,** *occurs:*
primo, de ipso incarnationis mysterio: the noun here is in the
ablative after **de** as is its emphatic modifier, **ipso,** *of the very mystery
of the incarnation* or *of the mystery itself of the incarnation,* **secundum
quod,** *according to which, insofar as.* **Deus** is the subject of the perfect
passive, **factus est,** *was made,* **homo,** *man,* **pro nostra salute:** this
preposition takes the ablative. *The first (consideration) is of the mystery
of the incarnation itself, according to which God became man for our
salvation.*

25   **Secunda,** with **consideratio** understood as well as the verb "to be,"
de his, *of those things,* **quae,** neuter nominative plural, **per isum
Salvatorem nostrum,** the noun and its possessive adjective in
agreement with **ipsum,** *Our Savior,* **idest Deum incarnatum,** *that is,
God Incarnate,* the case endings being governed by **ipsum** still, and
now two perfect passives, **sunt acta et passa,** from **agere** and the
deponent **patior, pati, passus sum.** The past participles which enter
into the formation of this tense—see Grammatical Appendix—are in
agreement with **quae.**

Lesson Twenty Two
Vademecum[1]

HERE IS A LITTLE *florilegium* or *bouquet* of Scriptural passages, the kind of one-liners whose English versions haunt the mind. You will want to add to this list as you become more familiar with the Vulgate version of the New Testament. You will want to use the new Vulgate—even Latin translations of the Bible seem to undergo constant change—which is available in a number of fairly inexpensive editions. It will be found in *Novum Testamentum Graece et Latine* edited by Gianfranco Nolli and published by Libreria Editrice Vaticana, Vatican City, 1986. The Latin alone can be had in the Nestle-Aland (Nestle was the original editor), *Novum Testamentum Latine,* edited by Kurt and Barbara Aland (Deutsche Bibelgesellschaft Stuttgart, 1992). Any bookseller will be happy to order either of these for you.

1. **Cum enim infirmor, tunc fortis sum.** (1 Cor 12.10)[2]

2. **Non enim erubesco evangelium.** (Rom 1.16)[3]

---

1 Such compounds are familiar in modern Spanish. *Vade* is a singular imperative from *vadere**. *(When an asterisk is attached to a word, that word will be found in the Vocabulary.)* The preposition **cum*** takes the accusative of **ego**. *Go with me* or *companion.*

2 **Cum enim* infirmor, tunc* fortis sum. Infirmor** is the first person singular, passive, of **infirmare** (1) The weakening or shaking signified in the active voice is turned on the speaker who thus can be said to ail or to be weakened. **Enim*** is a familiar conjunction, and **cum** another conjunction, here governing time. *For when I am weak.* **Tunc*,** and then **fortis**. nominative case of the adjective, which could be either masculine or feminine (**fortis, -e**), but in this case, given the subject of **sum**, is masculine. *Then I am strong.*

3 **Non* enim* erubesco evangelium*.** The only thing to take note of here is the verb, suggestive of redness and whose ending **-sco** indicates something in process, becoming. Thus **erubescere** (3) means *I grow red, I blush.* That such a

3. **Dominus meus adiutor est, non timebo; quid faciet mihi homo.** (Heb 13.6 = Ps 118.6)[4]

4. **Hic est Filius meus dilectus, in quo mihi complacui.** (Mt 3.17)[5]

5. **Non in pane solo vivet homo, sed in omni verbo, quod procedit de ore Dei.** (Mt 4.4)[6]

verb takes the accusative may surprise, since this suggests that one is blushing or reddening the gospel. But the meaning is what you would think: *For I am not ashamed of the gospel.*

4   **Dominus* meus* adiutor est.** The subject followed by a possessive adjective which agrees with its noun in gender, number, and case—that is, nominative singular masculine—followed by what seems to be a predicate adjective and the copula. The noun with which the possessive adjective goes is not **dominus** but **adjutor** (adjutor, adjutoris, m.), so the English order of the sentence could be **Dominus est meus adjutor.** *The Lord is my helper.* **Non* timebo*.** The verb is of course the first person singular future indicative of **timere*.** *I will not fear.* **Quid* faciet* mihi* homo*.** The neutral of **quis, quid** obviously cannot mean who; make it *what*. The verb is from **facere*,** a fourth conjugation, so you know that the form is third person singular future indicative. **Mihi** is the dative of **ego*.** *What will [any] man do to me.*

5   **Hic* est Filius* meus*, in* quo* mihi* complacui.** In the Vocabulary you will find **hic, haec, hoc,** a demonstrative adjective meaning *this.* Here it modifies **Filius** as does the possessive adjective, **meus*:** *This is my Son.* The verb is formed from the preposition **cum** and **placere** (2), and the form is first person singular perfect active, so *I have been pleased with.* **Mihi,** the dative, makes the verb reflexive. So we get something like *I myself have been pleased* or even *I have pleased myself.* The preposition **in** governs the ablative **quo.** *In whom I have been pleased.*

6   **Non* in* pane* solo* vivet homo*.** Vivere is third conjugation, so this is third person singular active; **homo** is the subject, and we can rearrange thus: **Homo non vivet in solo pane.** *Man does not live in (by) bread alone.* **Sed* in* omni* verbo*.** Isn't it nice to know that such a phrase is as easy as English for you now? *But in every word.* **Quod* procedit* de* ore Dei*.** Quod (qui, quae, quod) agrees with the neuter noun **verbum** which is the subject of third conjugation verb **procedere,** thus third person singular active. **Os, oris** n. (3), *mouth,* which you can add to the vocabulary; it is related to **ostium*,** *the door or mouth of a river,* hence

6. **Vos estis sal terrae; quod si sal evanuerit, in quo salietur?**
   (Mt 5.13)[7]

7. **Nemo potest duobus dominis servire.** (Mt 6.24)[8]

8. **Ierusalem, Ierusalem, quae occidis prophetas et lapidas eos, qui ad te missi sunt, quotiens volui congregare filios tuos, quemadmodum gallina congregat pullos suos sub alas, et noluistis.** (Mt. 23.37)[9]

Ostium, the mouth of the Tiber, the town where Augustine's mother Monica died. The town is now called Ostia. *That proceeds from the mouth of God.*

7   **Vos* estis* sal terrae*.** The personal pronoun is plural and governs the second person plural indicative active of **esse*** which links it with the predicate noun **sal, salis,** *salt. You are the salt of the earth* or perhaps better *of the world.* A metaphor, of course, suggesting a seasoning activity on the part of the followers of Christ; salt is a preservative as well, and this suggests instruments of salvation. **Quod** can modify the repeated **sal,** which governs **evanuerit,** a subjunctive from **evanescere** (3) which is introduced by **si,** if, which incredibly is not in the Vocabulary. *Which salt, if it should vanish* . . . **in quo salietur.** This fourth conjugation verb is not found in the usual manual dictionaries of classical Latin. The form is third person singular future passive. *In (with) what will it be salted?*

8   **Nemo* potest* duobus* dominis* servire. Servire** (4) *to work for, slave for, serve,* takes the dative rather than the accusative as its object. **Dominis** is a dative plural, modified by the dative plural form of **duo,** which you will find in the list of numerals. The infinitive **servire** follows on **potest,** the third person singular present active tense of **posse.** The subject is the noun **nemo.** *No man can serve two masters.*

9   **Ierusalem, Ierusalem.** The name of the city used vocatively, since Christ is addressing it, or more accurately, its inhabitants. The relative pronoun **quae** tells us that the word **Ierusalem** is feminine, which is usually the case with cities. **Quae* occidis* prophetas* et* lapidas eos*. Occidere** is fourth declension and this is third person singular indicative active. **Propheta** is a feminine form, but inclusive (if there were female prophets who were killed and stoned). **Eos** is accusative plural masculine, indicating the prophets are masculine, whatever the form of the noun.

   Lapidare (1) is a verb formed from **lapidum*.** *Jerusalem, Jerusalem, [you] who kill the prophets and stone them.* **Qui ad te missi sunt.** The masculine relative pronoun, a nomina-

9. **Non est propheta sine honore, nisi in patria sua et in cognatione sua et in domo sua.** (Mc 6.4)[10]

10. **Quae sunt Caesaris, reddite Caesari et, quae sunt Dei, Deo.** (Mc 12.17)[11]

11. **Nunc autem manet fides, spes, caritas, tria haec; maior autem ex his est caritas.** (1 Cor 13.13)[12]

tive plural, picks up on prophets and governs the verb **missi sunt,** a perfect passive from **mittere*.** The preposition **ad*** governs the personal **te** (= Jersualem). *Who were sent to thee.* **Quotiens volui congregare filios tuos. Quotiens,** adverb, *how often;* **volui** is the first person perfect of **volere** (2). The infinitive **congregare** is formed from the noun **grex, gregis,** *flock,* not inappropriate here; **filios* tuos*,** accusative plural, masculine to agree with **filios.** *How many time I wished to gather your children.* **Quemadmodum gallina congregat pullos suos sub alas.** An adverb compounded of three words, **quem ad modum, ad modum,** *in the manner,* *à la mode,* **ad quem modum,** *in that manner = as.* **Gallina** (1) is the subject of **congregat,** third person singular, whose object is the accusative plural, **gallinos suos*.** The preposition **sub** takes the accusative of **ala, alae,** f. *As a hen gathers her chicks under her wings.* **Et noluistis.** This is the second person plural perfect active of the irregular verb **nolle*.** *And you would not.*

10   **Non* est* propheta* sine* honore.** That last word is the ablative singular of **honor, honoris,** m., governed by the preposition **sine.** *A prophet is not without honor.* **Nisi* in* patria sua*.** *Unless in his own country.* **Et in cognatione sua et domo sua.** On **cognatio, cognationis,** f. see in the Vocabulary **cognatus. Domus*** is feminine, hence **sua.** These phrases continue to be governed by **nisi.** *Unless among his own kin and in his own house.*

11   **Quae* sunt* Caesaris, reddite* Caesari et* quae* sunt* Dei*, Deo*.** Only the proper name Caesar is not in your Vocabulary. **Caesar, Caesaris, Caesari, Caesarem, Caesari.** So we have a genitive and a dative. **Quae** is a collective, meaning *what, those things, that which.* **Reddite** is the imperative of **reddere*.** We have the genitive and dative of **Deus** to complement those of **Caesar.** *What is Caesar's, render to Caesar, and what is God's to God.*

12   **Nunc* autem* manet* fides, spes*, caritas, tria* haec*.** The verb is the third person singular indicative active of **manere,** and has as its subject, collectively or distributively, **fides, spes, caritas.** Both **spes** and **fides** are fifth declension; **caritas** is third. **Haec** is nominative feminine of the demon-

12. **Illum oportet crescere, me autem minui** (Jn 3.30)[13]

---

strative, and **tria** the neuter form of the numeral. *Now then (however) there are these three, faith, hope, charity.* **Major autem ex his est caritas.** The comparative form of the adjective **magnus, magna,** here feminine to agree with its noun. Since it is contrasted with the two other theological virtues, this is taken as a superlative. The preposition **ex** takes the ablative, and **his** is the ablative plural of the demonstrative. *But the greatest of these is charity.*

13   **Illum* oportet crescere*, me* autem* minui*.** The irregular and impersonal verb **oportet** takes an accusative with an infinitive, and it covers both **crescere** and the contrasting **minui,** a passive infinitive. John the Baptist is referring to Christ. *He must increase, but I must decrease.*

Grammatical Appendix

Grammar

The Conjugation of Verbs

The verb *to be* (esse)

THE CONJUGATION OF ESSE **whose principal parts are sum**, present indicative, **esse**, present infinitive, **fui**, perfect indicative, **futurus**, future participle

ACTIVE VOICE
INDICATIVE MOOD
Present

sum, *I am*   **sumus,** *we are*
es, *you are*   **estis,** *you are*
est, *he, she, it is*   **sunt,** *they are*

Imperfect

eram, *I was*   **eramus,** *we were*
eras, *you were*   **eratis,** *you were*
erat, *he was*   **erant,** *they were*

Future

ero, *I shall be*   **erimus,** *we shall be*
eris, *you shall be*   **eritis,** *you shall be*
erit, *he shall be*   **erunt,** *they shall be*

Perfect

fui, *I was, have been*   **fuimus,** *we have been*
fuisti, *you have been*   **fuistis,** *you have been*
fuit, *he has been*   **fuerunt,** *they have been*

Pluperfect

fueram, *I had been*   **fueramus,** *we had been*
fueras, *you had been*   **fueratis,** *you had been*
fuerat, *he had been*   **fuerant,** *they had been*

Future Perfect

fuero, *I shall have been*   **fuerimus,** *we shall have been*
fueris, *you will have been*   **fueritis,** *you shall have been*
fuerit, *he will have been*   **fuerint,** *they shall have been*

SUBJUNCTIVE MOOD
Present

sim, *may I be*   **simus,** *let us be*
sis, *may you be*   **sitis,** *may you be*
sit, *may he be*   **sint,** *let them be*

Imperfect

essem, *I should be*   **essemus,** *we should be*
esses, *you would be*   **essetis,** *you would be*
esset, *he would be*   **essent,** *they would be*

Perfect

fuerim, *I may have been*   **fuerimus,** *we may have been*
fueris, *you may have been*   **fueritis,** *you may have been*
fuerit, *he may have been*   **fuerint,** *they may have been*

Pluperfect

fuissem, *I should have been*   **fuissemus,** *we should have been*
fuisses, *you would have been*   **fuissetis,** *you would have been*
fuisset, *he would have been*   **fuissent,** *they would have been*

IMPERATIVE MOOD

Present: **es,** *you be!*   **este,** *you be!*
Future: **esto,** *you shall be!*   **estote,** *you shall be!*
             esto, *he shall be!*   **sunto,** *they shall be!*

INFINITIVE

Present: **esse,** *to be*
Perfect: **fuisse,** *to have been*
Future: **futurus esse,** *to be about to be*

FIRST CONJUGATION
ACTIVE VOICE
Principal Parts: **amo, amare, amavi, amatus**

INDICATIVE MOOD
Present

amo, *I love*   **amamus,** *we love*
amas, *you love*   **amatis,** *you love*
amat, *he loves*   **amant,** *they love*

Imperfect

amabam, *I was loving*   **amabamus,** *we were loving*
amabas, *you were loving*   **amabatis,** *you were loving*
amabat, *he was loving*   **amabant,** *they were loving*

Future

amabo, *I shall love*   **amabimus,** *we shall love*
amabis, *you will love*   **amabitis,** *you will love*
amabit, *he will love*   **amabunt,** *they will love*

Perfect

amavi, *I loved*   **amavimus,** *we loved*
amavisti, *you loved*   **amavistis,** *you loved*
amavit, *he loved*   **amaverunt,** *they loved*

Pluperfect

amaveram, *I had loved*   **amaveramus,** *we had loved*
amaveras, *you had loved*   **amaveratis,** *you had loved*
amaverat, *he had loved*   **amaverant,** *they had loved*

Future Perfect

amavero, *I shall have loved*   **amaverimus,** *we shall have loved*
amaveris, *you will have loved*   **amaveritis,** *you will have loved*
amaverit, *he will have loved*   **amaverint,** *they will have loved*

SUBJUNCTIVE
Present

amem, *may I love*   **amemus,** *let us love*
ames, *may you love*   **ametis,** *may you love*
amet, *may he love*   **ament,** *let them love*

Imperfect

amarem, *I should love*	**amaremus,** *we should love*
amares, *you would love*	**amaretis,** *you would love*
amaret, *he would love*	**amarent,** *they would love*

Perfect

amaverim, *I may have loved*	**amaverimus,** *we may have loved*
amaveris, *you may have loved*	**amaveritis,** *you may have loved*
amaverit, *he may have loved*	**amaverint,** *they may have loved*

Pluperfect

amavissem, *I should have loved*	**amavissemus,** *we should have loved*
amavisses, *you would have loved*	**amavissetis,** *you would have loved*
amavisset, *he would have loved*	**amavissent,** *they would have loved*

IMPERATIVE

Present:	**ama,** *love!*	**amate,** *love!*
Future:	**amato,** *you will love!*	**amatote,** *you will love!*

INFINITIVE

Present:	**amare,** *to love*
Perfect:	**amavisse,** *to have loved*
Future:	**amaturus esse,** *to be about to love*

PARTICIPLE

Present:	**amans,** *loving*
Future:	**amaturus,** *about to love*

GERUND

amandus -a, -um

PASSIVE VOICE

Principal Parts: **amor   amari   amatus sum**

INDICATIVE

Present *(I am loved, etc.)*

amor	amamur
amaris	amamini
amatur	amantur

Imperfect *(I was loved...)*

amabar	amabamur
amabaris	amabimini
amabatur	amabantur

(I will be loved...)

amabor	amabimur
amaberis	amabimini
amabitur	amabuntur

(I was loved...)

amatus sum	amati sumus
amatus es	amati estis
amatus est	amati sunt

Pluperfect *(I had been loved...)*

amatus eram	amati eramus
amatus eras	amati eratis
amatus erat	amati erant

Future Perfect *(I will have been loved...)*

amatus ero	amati erimus
amatus eris	amati eritis
amatus erit	amati erunt

SUBJUNCTIVE
Present *(May I be loved...)*

amer	amemur
ameris	amemini
ametur	amentur

Imperfect *(I should be loved...)*

amarer	amaremur
amareris	amaremini
amaretur	amarentur

Perfect *(I may have been loved...)*

amatus sim	amati simus
amatus sis	amati sitis
amatus sit	amati sint

Pluperfect *(I should have been loved...)*

amatus essem	amati essemus
amatus esses	amati essetis
amatus esset	amati essent

IMPERATIVE

Present: **amare,** *be loved!*   **amamini,** *be loved!*
Future: **amator,** *be ye loved!*

INFINITIVE

Present: **amari,** *to be loved*
Perfect: **amatus esse,** *to have been loved*

PARTICIPLE

Perfect: **amatus,** *having been loved*
Gerundive: **amandus,** *to be loved*

SECOND CONJUGATION
Principal Parts: **moneo, monere, monui, monitus**

INDICATIVE MOOD
Present *(I warn, you warn...)*

moneo	monemus
mones	monetis
monet	monent

Imperfect *(I was warning...)*

monebam	monebamus
monebas	monebatis
monebat	monebant

Future *(I will warn...)*

monebo	monebimus
monebis	monebitis
monebit	monebunt

Perfect *(I warned...)*

monui	monuimus
monuisti	monuistis
monuit	monuerunt

Pluperfect *(I had warned...)*

monueram	monueramus
moneras	monueratis
monuerat	monuerant

Future Perfect *(I will have warned...)*

monuero	monuerimus
monueris	monueritis
monuerit	monuerint

SUBJUNCTIVE
Present *(May I warn...)*

moneam	moneamus
moneas	moneatis
moneat	moneant

Imperfect *(I would warn...)*

monerem	moneremus
moneres	moneretis
moneret	monerent

Perfect *(I may have warned...)*

monuerim	monuerimus
monueris	monueritis
monuerit	monuerint

Pluperfect *(I would have warned...)*

monuissem	monuissemus
monisses	monuissetis
monuisset	monuissent

IMPERATIVE

Present:	mone *(Warn!)*	monete *(Warn!)*	
Future:	moneto	monetote	

INFINITIVE

Present:	monere, *to warn*
Perfect:	monuisse, *to have warned*
Future:	moniturus esse, *to be about to warn*

PARTICIPLE

Present: **monens,** *warning*
Future: **moniturus,** *about to warn*
Gerund: **monendus**

PASSIVE VOICE
INDICATIVE MOOD

Present *(I am warned...)*

moneor	monemur
moneris	monemini
monetur	monentur

Imperfect *(I was warned...)*

monebar	monebamur
monebaris	monebamini
monebatur	monebantur

Future *(I will be warned...)*

monebor	monebimur
moneberis	monebimini
monebitur	monebuntur

Perfect *(I was warned...)*

monitus sum	moniti sumus
monitus es	moniti estis
monitus est	moniti sunt

Pluperfect *(I had been warned...)*

monitus eram	moniti eramus
monitus eras	moniti eratis
monitus erat	moniti erant

Future Perfect *(I will have been warned...)*

monitus ero	moniti erimus
monitus eris	moniti eritis
monitus erit	moniti erunt

SUBJUNCTIVE
Present (*May I be warned...*)

monear	moneamur
monearis	moneamini
moneatur	moneantur

Imperfect (*I would be warned...*)

monerer	moneremur
monereris	moneremini
moneretur	monerentur

Perfect (*I may have been warned...*)

monitus sim	moniti simus
monitus sis	moniti sitis
monitus sit	moniti sint

Pluperfect (*I would have been warned...*)

monitus essem	moniti essemus
moniturs esses	moniti essetis
monitus esset	moniti essent

IMPERATIVE

Present:	monere	monemini
Future:	monetor	

INFINITIVE

Present:	moneri
Perfect:	monitus esse
Future:	monitus iri

PARTICIPLE

Perfect:	monitus
Gerundive:	monendus

THIRD CONJUGATION
ACTIVE VOICE
Principal Parts: **rego, regere, regi, rectus**

INDICATIVE MOOD
Present *(I rule...)*

rego	regimus
regis	regitis
regit	regunt

Imperfect (I was ruling...)

regebam	regebamus
regebas	regebatis
regebat	regebant

Future (I will rule...)

regam	regemus
reges	regetis
reget	regent

Perfect *(I ruled...)*

rexi	reximus
rexisti	rexistis
rexit	rexerunt

Pluperfect *(I had ruled...)*

rexeram	rexeramus
rexeras	rexeratis
rexerat	rexerant

Future Perfect *(I will have ruled...)*

rexero	rexerimus
rexeris	rexeritis
rexerit	rexerint

SUBJUNCTIVE
Present *(May I rule...)*

regam	regamus
regas	regatis
regat	regant

Imperfect *(I should rule...)*

regerem	regeremus
regeres	regeretis
regeret	regerent

Perfect *(I may have ruled...)*

rexerim	**rexerimus**
rexeris	**rexeritis**
rexerit	**rexerint**

Pluperfect *(I would have ruled...)*

rexissem	**rexissemus**
rexisses	**rexissetis**
rexisset	**rexissent**

IMPERATIVE

Present:	**rege,** *rule!*	**regite,** *rule!*
Future:	**regito,** *you shall rule!*	**regitote,** *you shall rule!*

INFINITIVE

Present:	**regere,** *to rule*
Perfect:	**rexisse,** *to have ruled*
Future:	**recturus esse,** *to be about to rule*

PARTICIPLE

Present:	**regens,** *ruling*
Future:	**recturus,** *about to rule*
Gerund:	**regendum**

PASSIVE VOICE
Principal Parts: **regor, regi, rectus sum**

INDICATIVE MOOD

Present *(I am ruled...)*

regor	**regimur**
regeris	**regimini**
regitur	**reguntur**

Imperfect *(I was ruled...)*

regebar	**regebamur**
regebaris	**regebamini**
regebatur	**regebantur**

Future *(I will be ruled...)*

regar	regemur
regeris	regemini
regetur	regentur

Perfect *(I was ruled...)*

rectus sum	recti sumus
rectus es	recti estis
rectus est	recti sunt

Pluperfect *(I had been ruled...)*

rectus eram	recti eramus
rectus eras	recti eratis
rectus erat	recti erant

Future Perfect *(I will have been ruled...)*

rectus ero	recti erimus
rectus eris	recti eritis
rectus erit	recti erunt

SUBJUNCTIVE

Present *(May I be ruled...)*

regar	regamur
regaris	regamini
regatur	regantur

Imperfect *(I would be ruled...)*

regerer	regeremur
regereris	regeremini
regeretur	regerentur

Perfect *(I may have been ruled...)*

rectus sim	recti simus
rectus sis	recti sitis
rectus sit	recti sint

Pluperfect *(I would have been ruled...)*

rectus essem	recti essemus
rectus esses	recti essetis
rectus esset	recti essent

IMPERATIVE

Present: **regere,** *be ruled* **regimini,** *be ruled*
Future: **regitor,** *you shall be ruled!*

INFINITIVE

Present: **regi,** *to be ruled*
Perfect: **rectus esse,** *to have been ruled*
Future: **rectum iri,** *to be about to be ruled*

PARTICIPLE

Perfect: **rectus,** *having been ruled*
Gerundive: **regendus,** *ought to be ruled*

FOURTH CONJUGATION
ACTIVE VOICE
Audio, *I hear*
Principal Parts: **audio, audire, audivi, auditus**

INDICATIVE MOOD
Present Tense (*I hear...*)

audio	audimus
audis	auditis
audit	audiunt

Imperfect (*I was hearing...*)

audiebam	audiebamus
audiebas	audiebatis
audiebat	audiebant

Future (*I will hear...*)

audiam	audiemus
audies	audietis
audiet	audient

Perfect (*I heard...*)

audivi	audivimus
audivisti	audivistis
audivit	audiverunt

Pluperfect *(I had heard...)*

audiveram	audiveramus
audiveras	audiveratis
audiverat	audiverant

Future Perfect *(I will have heard...)*

audivero	audiverimus
auiveris	audiveritis
audiverit	audiverint

SUBJUNCTIVE
Present *(May I hear...)*

audiam	audiamus
audias	audiatis
audiat	audiant

Imperfect *(I should hear...)*

audirem	audiremus
audires	audiretis
audiret	audirent

Perfect *(I may have heard...)*

audiverim	audiverimus
audiveris	audiveritis
audiverit	audiverint

Pluperfect *(I should have heard...)*

audivissem	audivissemus
audivisses	audivissetis
audivisset	audivissent

IMPERATIVE

Present:	audi	audite
Future:	audito	auditote

INFINITIVE

Present:	audire
Perfect:	audivisse
Future:	auditurus esse

PARTICIPLE

Present: **audiens**
Future: **auditurus**
Gerund: **audiendum**

PASSIVE VOICE
Principal Parts: **audior, audiri, auditus sum**

INDICATIVE
Present *(I am heard...)*

audior	audimur
audiris	audimini
auditur	audiuntur

Imperfect *(I was heard...)*

audiebar	audiebamur
audiebaris	audiebamini
audiebatur	audiebantur

Future *(I will be heard...)*

audiar	audiemur
audieris	audiemini
audietur	audientur

Perfect *(I was heard...)*

auditus sum	auditi sumus
auditis es	auditi estis
auditus est	auditi sunt

Pluperfect *(I had been heard...)*

auditus eram	auditi eramus
auditus eras	auditi eratis
auditus erat	auditi erant

Future Perfect *(I will have been heard...)*

auditus ero	auditi erimus
auditus eris	auditi eritis
auditus erit	auditi erunt

SUBJUNCTIVE
Present *(May I be heard...)*

audiar	audiamur
audiaris	audiamini
audiatur	audiantur

Imperfect *(I would be heard...)*

audirer	audiremur
audireris	audiremini
audiretur	audirentur

Perfect *(I may have been heard...)*

auditus sim	auditi simus
auditus sis	auditi sitis
auditus sit	auditi sint

Pluperfect *(I would have been heard...)*

auditus essem	auditi essemus
auditus esses	auditi essetis
auditus esset	auditi essent

IMPERATIVE

Present:	audire	audimini
Future:	auditor	

INFINITIVE

Present:	audiri
Perfect:	auditus esse
Future:	auditum iri

PARTICIPLE

Perfect:	auditus
Gerundive:	audiendum

The Declension of Nouns

THERE ARE FIVE DECLENSIONS in Latin; they can be recognized by the final letter of their stem and by the ending of the genitive singular.

First	a	-ae
Second	o	-i
Third	i	-is
	(or consonant)	
Fourth	u	-us
Fifth	e	-ei

FIRST DECLENSION
porta, -ae, *gate*

	Singular	Plural
Nominative	porta	portae
Genitive	portae	portarum
Dative	portae	portis
Accusative	portam	portas
Ablative	porta	portis
Vocative	porta	portae

SECOND DECLENSION
bellum, -i, neuter, *war*

	Singular	Plural
Nominative	bellum	bella
Genitive	belli	bellorum
Dative	bello	bellis
Accusative	bellum	bella
Ablative	bello	bellis
Vocative	bellum	bella

hortus, -i, masculine, *garden*

	Singular	Plural
Nominative	**hortus**	**horti**
Genitive	**horti**	**hortorum**
Dative	**horto**	**hortis**
Accusative	**hortum**	**hortos**
Ablative	**horto**	**hortis**
Vocative	**horte**	**horti**

puer, -i, masculine, *boy*

	Singular	Plural
Nominative	**puer**	**pueri**
Gentitive	**pueri**	**puerorum**
Dative	**puero**	**pueris**
Accusative	**puerum**	**pueros**
Ablative	**puero**	**pueris**
Vocative	**puer**	**pueri**

THIRD DECLENSION

This is a very commodious declension, accommodating nouns that end in a, e, i, o, y. c, l, n, r, s, t, x. What they all have in common are the same case endings after the nominative singular—these differ in the way just mentioned.

	Singular	Plural
Nominative	X	**-es**
Genitive	**-is**	**-um**
Dative	**-i**	**-ibus**
Accusative	**-em**	**-es**
Ablative	**-e**	**-ibus**
Vocative	X	**-es**

I will illustrate the Third Declension with two nouns:

dux, ducis, leader

	Singular	Plural
Nominative	**dux**	**duces**
Genitive	**ducis**	**ducum**
Dative	**duci**	**ducibus**
Accusative	**ducem**	**duces**
Ablative	**duce**	**ducibus**
Vocative.	**dux**	**duces**

leo, -onis, masculine, *lion*

	Singular	Plural
Nominative	leo	leones
Genitive	leonis	leonum
Dative	leoni	leonibus
Accusative	leonem	leones
Ablative	leone	leonibus
Vocative	leo	leones

FOURTH DECLENSION

fructus, -us, masuculine, *fruit*

	Singular	Plural
Nominative	fructus	fructus
Genitive	fructus	fructuum
Dative	fructui	fructibus
Accusative	fructum	fructus
Ablative	fructu	fructus
Vocative	fructus	fructus

FIFTH DECLENSION

dies, diei, masculine, *day*

	Singular	Plural
Nominative	dies	dies
Genitive	diei	dierum
Dative	diei	diebus
Accusative	diem	dies
Ablative	die	diebus
Vocative	dies	dies

Pronouns

DEMONSTRATIVES

hic, *this*

	Masc.	*Fem.*	*Neut.*
Singular			
Nominative	hic	haec	hoc
Genitive	huius	huius	huius
Dative	huic	huic	huic
Accusative	hunc	hanc	hoc
Ablative	hoc	hac	hoc
Plural			
Nominative	hi	hae	haec
Genitive	horum	harum	horum
Dative	his	his	his
Accusative	hos	has	haec
Ablative	his	his	his

ille, *that*

	Masc.	*Fem.*	*Neut.*
Singular			
Nominative	ille	illa	illud
Genitive	illius	illius	illius
Dative	illi	illi	illi
Accusative	illum	illam	illud
Ablative	illo	illa	illo
Plural			
Nominative	illi	illae	illa
Genitive	illorum	illarum	illorum
Dative	illis	illis	illis
Accusative	illos	illas	illa
Ablative	illis	illis	illis

is, *this, that, he, she, it*

	Masc.	Fem.	Neut.
Singular			
Nominative	is	ea	id
Genitive	eius	eius	eius
Dative	ei	ei	ei
Accusative	eum	eam	id
Ablative	eo	ea	eo

	Masc.	Fem.	Neut.
Plural			
Nominative	ii	eae	ea
Genitive	eorum	earum	eorum
Dative	eis	eis	eis
Accusative	eos	eas	ea
Ablative	eis	eis	eis

idem, *the same*

	Masc.	Fem.	Neut.
Singular			
Nominative	idem	eadem	idem
Genitive	eiusdem	eiusdem	eiusdem
Dative	eidem	eidem	eidem
Accusative	eundem	eandem	idem
Ablative	eodem	eadem	eodem

	Masc.	Fem.	Neut.
Plural			
Nominative	eidem	eaedem	eadem
Genitive	eorundem	earundem	eorundem
Dative	eisdem	eisdem	eisdem
Accusative	eosdem	easdem	eadem
Ablative	eisdem	eisdem	eisdem

RELATIVE
qui, *who, which*

	Masc.	Fem.	Neut.
Singular			
Nominative	qui	quae	quod
Genitive	cuius	cuius	cuius
Dative	cui	cui	cui
Accusative	quem	quam	quod
Ablative	quo	qua	quo

	Masc.	*Fem.*	*Neut.*
		Plural	
Nominative	qui	quae	quae
Genitive	quorum	quarum	quorum
Dative	quibus	quibus	quibus
Accusative	quos	quas	quae
Ablative	quibus	quibus	quibus

INTERROGATIVE
quis, *who?*

	Masc.	*Fem.*	*Neut.*
		Singular	
Nominative	quis	quis	quid
Genitive	cuius	cuius	cuius
Dative	cui	cui	cui
Accusative	quem	quem	quid
Ablative	quo	quo	quo

	Masc.	*Fem.*	*Neut.*
		Plural	
Nominative	qui	quae	quae
Genitive	quorum	quorum	quorum
Dative	quibus	quibus	quibus
Accusative	quos	quas	quae
Ablative	quibus	quibus	quibus

INTENSIVE
ipse, *himself...*

	Masc.	*Fem.*	*Neut.*
		Singular	
Nominative	ipse	ipsa	ipsum
Genitive	ipsius	ipsius	ipsius
Dative	ipsi	ipsi	ipsi
Accusative	ipsum	ipsam	ipsum
Ablative	ipso	ipsa	ipso

		Plural	
Nominative	ipsi	ipsae	ipsa
Genitive	ipsorum	ipsarum	ipsorum
Dative	ipsis	ipsis	ipsis
Accusative	ipsos	ipsas	ipsa
Ablative	ipsis	ipsis	ipsis

Comparison of Adjectives

Regular

longus, -, -um, *long*	**longior, -ius**	**longissimus, -a, -um**
acer, acris, acre, *sharp*	**acrior, -ius**	**acerrimus, -a, -um**
facilis, -e, *easy*	**facilior, -ius**	**facillimus, -a, -um**
felix, *happy*	**felicior, -ius**	**felicissimus, -a, -um**
fortis, *brave*	**fortior, -ius**	**fortissimus, -a, -um**
pulcher, -ra, -rum, *pretty*	**pulchrior, -ius**	**pulcherrimus, -a, -um**
sapiens, *wise*	**sapientior, -ius**	**sapientissimus, -a, -um**

Irregular

bonus, -a, -um, *good*	**melior, -ius**	**optimus, -a, -um**
magnus, -a, -um, *large*	**maior, -ius**	**maximus, -a, -um**
malus, -a, -um, *bad*	**peior, -ius**	**pessimus, -a, -um**
multus, -a, -um, *much*	**plus**	**plurimus, -a, -um**
parvus, -a, -um, *little*	**minor, minus**	**minimus, -a, -um**

Numerals

	Cardinals	Ordinals
1	unus, -a, -um	primus, -a, um
2	duo, duae, duo	secundus, -a, -um
3	tres, tria	tertius, -a, -um
4	quattuor	quartus, -a, -um
5	quinque	quintus, -a, -um
6	sex	sextus, -a, -um
7	septem	septimus, -a,-um
8	octo	octavus, -a, -um
9	novem	nonus, -a, -um
10	decem	decimus, -a, -um
11	undecim	undecimus, -a, -um
12	duodecim	duodecimus, -a, -um
13	tredecim	tertius decimus
14	quattuordecim	quartus decimus
15	quindecim	quintus decimus
16	sedecim	sextus decimus
17	septendecim	septimus decimus
18	duodeviginti	duodevicesimus
19	undeviginti	undevicesimus
20	viginti	vicesimus
21	viginti unus	vicesimus primus
30	triginta	trecesimus
40	quadraginta	quadragesimus
50	quinquaginta	quinquagesimus
60	sexaginta	sexagesimus
70	septuaginta	septuagesimus
80	octoginta	octogesimus
90	nonaginta	nonagesimus
100	centum	centesimus
200	ducenti, -ae, -a	ducentesimus
300	trecenti	trecentesimus
400	quadringenti	quadringentesimus
500	quingenti	quingentesimus
600	sescenti	sescentesimus
700	septingenti	septingentesimus
800	octingenti	octingentesimus
900	nongenti	nongentesimus
1000	mille	millesimus

Vocabulary

The number in parenthesis indicates the declension, in the case of nouns, and the conjugation, in the case of regular verbs.

A

a, prep., *away, from*
abluere (3), *to wash*
abnegare (1), *to deny*
abscindere (3), *to tear off, wrench away*
abscondere (3), *to hide, conceal*
absumere (3), *to lessen, destroy, consume*
abundanter, adv., *abundantly*
accedere (3), *to arrive at, reach*
accidere (3), *to come about, happen*
accipere (3), *to take or receive*
acervare (1), *to pile up*
acies, -ei, f. (5), *army*
aculeus, -i, m. (2), *sting*
acus, -us, f. (4), *needle*
ad, prep., *to or toward*, with the accusative
adesse, *to be present*
adferre (ad + fero, ferre, tuli, latus), *to bring forward*
adhuc, adv., *still*
adjungere (3), *to join to, adjoin*
admiror, dep. (1), *to wonder at*
adornare (1), *to adorn*
advenire, vb., *to come, arrive*
adversum, prep., *against*
advocata, -ae, f. (1), *intercessor*
aestas, -tatis, f. (3), *summer*
aestimare (1), *to think, reckon*
aeternus, -a, -um, adj., *eternal*
agmen, -inis, n. (3), *crowd, mass*
aio, ait, defective vb., *to say, affirm*

alioquin, adv., *otherwise*
aliquando, adv., *sometimes*
aliquatenus, adv., *to a certain degree*
alter, -era, -um, adj., *other*
amabilis, -e, adj., *loveable*
amare (1), *to love*
amaritudo, -dinis, f. (3), *bitterness*
ambulare (1), *to walk*
ancilla, n. (1), *servant, handmaid*
angelus, angeli, *angel*
anima, animae, f. (1), *soul*
annuntiare (1), *to announce, declare*
annus, -i, m. (2), *year*
ante, prep., *before*
aperire (4), *to open*
apostolus, -i, m. (2), *apostle*
appetere (3), *to desire, seek*
approximare (1), *to draw near*
apud, prep., *at, near, by, with*
aqua, -ae, f. (1), *water*
arbor, -oris, f. (3), *tree*
ardor, -is, m. (3), *heat, ardor*
ascendere, (3), *to ascend, go up*
ascensio, -onis, f. (3), *ascent*
atque, *also*
attendere (3), *to await*
attingere (3), *to reach, attain*
audire (3), *to hear*
auditio, -onis, f. (3), *listening, hearing*
auris, -is, f. (3), *ear*
aurora, -ae, f. (1), *dawn*
aurum, -i, n. (2), *gold*

autem, *however*
ave, imperative of **aveo,** *hail*
avellere (3), *to tear away*

B

beatitudo, -tudinis, f. (3),
    happiness
beatus, beata, beatum, *blessed*
benedicere (3), *to bless*
benedictus, benedicta,
    benedictum, adj., *blessed*
bibere (3), *to drink*
bonus, bona, bonum, *good*
brachium, -i, (2), *arm*
brevitas, -tatis, f. (3), *brevity*

C

cadaver, -is, n. (3), *corpse*
cadere (3), *to fall*
caecus, -a, -um, adj., *blind*
caelum. see **coelum**
camelum, -i, n. (2), *camel*
camus, -i, m. (2), *bit*
candere (2), *to shine, to shine*
    whitely
cantare (1), *to sing*
capax, -acis, adj., *capable*
caput, caputis, n. (3), *head*
caro, carnis, f. (3), *flesh*
castrum, -i, n. (2), *fort, camp*
catholicus, -a, -um, *universal,*
    catholic
causa, -ae, f. (1), *cause*
celebrare (1), *to celebrate*
cena, -ae, f. (1), *banquet*
certamen, -minis, n. (3), *contest*
certare (1), *to contest, contend,*
    struggle
chorus, -i, m. (2), *choir*
Christus, Christi, *Christ*
circumdare (1), *to surround*
circumspicere (3), *to look around*

claritas, -tatis, f. (3), *clarity,*
    brightness
clarus, -a, -um, adj., *clear*
claudus, -a, -um, adj., *lame,*
    crippled
clemens, clementis, adj., *mild,*
    kind
coelum, coeli, n., *heaven*
coelum. cf. **caelum**
cognatus, -a, -um, *related*
cognitio, -onis, f. (3), *knowledge*
cognoscere (3), *to know*
columba, -ae, f. (1), *dove, pigeon*
commendare (1), *to commend*
communio, -ionis, f. (3),
    communion, sharing
commutatio, -onis, f. (3),
    exchange
complementum, -i, (2), *what*
    completes or fulfills
complere (2), *to complete, fill up*
compunctio, -onis, f. (3),
    compunction
compungere (3), *to prick, needle,*
    puncture
concipere, (4), *to conceive*
confessio, -onis, f. (3), *confession*
confiteor, dep. (2), *to confess*
confundere (3), *to disorder,*
    confuse
congruere (3), *to coincide,*
    correspond
consequenter, adv., *following on,*
    consequently
consequor, dep. (3), *to pursue*
conservare (1), *to preserve*
considerare (1), *to consider*
consistere (3), *to consist of*
conspicuus, -a, -um, adj., *visible*
conspicere (3), *to behold, descry*
constringere (3), *to restrain*
consulere (3), *to advise*
consumere (3), *to use up*
contemnere (3), *to think meanly*
    of, despise

contemplor, dep. (1), *to contemplate, gaze upon*

contere (3), *to crush*

continuo, adv., *at once, immediately*

conveniens, adj, *proper, fitting*

convivium, -i, n. (2), *banquet*

convolvere (3), *to roll up*

cooperari, dep. (1), *to work with*

copiosus, -a, -um, adj., *abundant*

cor, cordis, n. (3), *heart*

coram, prep., *before, in thepresence of*

corona, -ae, f. (1), *crown*

coronare (1), *to crown*

coronatio, -onis, f. (3), *crowning*

corpus, -oris, n. (3), *body*

corrumpare (1), *to corrupt*

creator, creatoris, m. (3), *creator*

credere, (3), *to believe*

crescere (4), *to grow up, increase*

crimen, -inis, n. (3), *accusation, crime*

cruciare (1), *to torment*

crucifigere (3), *to crucify*

crudelis, -e, adj., *cruel*

crux, crucis, f. (3), *cross*

cum, prep., *with*

cunctus, -a, -um, adj., *all*

cupiditas, cupiditatis, f. (3), *eager desire*

curare (1), *to care, to heal*

curatio, -onis, f. (3), *attention, a taking care*

custodire (4), *to shelter*

custos, -odis, m. (3), *sentry, guard*

D

dare, (1), *to give*

de, prep., *from, of*

debere (2), *to owe*

debilis, -e, adj., *weak*

debitor, debitoris, m., *debtor*

debitum, debiti, n. *debt*

decies, adv., *ten times*

deficere (3), *to fail, fade*

deinceps, adv., *one after the other, successively*

delictum, -i, n. (2), *fault, crime*

denarium, -i, n. (2), *denarium, coin*

depingere (3), *to depict, portray*

deponere (3), *to put down, depose*

deputare (1), *to prune, cut off, put off*

descendere (3), *to come down, descend*

descensus, -us, m. (4), *descent*

descriptio, -onis, f. (3), *representation in signs*

destruere (3), *to destroy*

detorquere (2), *to turn away*

detrimentum, -i, n. (2), *loss*

Deus, dei, n. m., *God*

devincere (3), *to conquer, subjugate*

dexter, dextra, dextrum, *right*

dextera, -ae, (1), *right hand*

diabolus, -i, m. (2), *devil*

dicere (3), *to say*

dies, -ei, m. f. (5), *day*

difficilis, -e, adj., *difficult*

dignari, dep. (1), *to esteem, honor, deem*

dignatio, -onis, f. (3), *favor*

dignus, -a, -um, adj., *worthy*

dilatio, -onis, f. (3), *delay, deferral*

diligenter, adv., *diligently, lovingly*

diluvium, -i, n. (2), *flood*

dimidium, -i, n. (2), *half, midway*

dimittere (3), *to forgive, dismiss*

discere (3), *to learn*

discipulus, -i, m. (2), *learner, disciple*

disperdere (3), *to destroy, ruin*

dispergere (3), *to dismiss, disperse*

diu, adv., *for a long time*

dives, divitis, adj., *rich*
divinus, -a, -um, adj., *divine*
divisio, -onis, f. (3), *division*
docere (2), *to teach*
documentum, -i, n. (2), *example, proof*
dolere (2), *to suffer pain*
dolorosus, -a, -um, adj., *sorrowful*
dolus, -i, m. (2), *deceit, guilt*
dominare (1), *to rule*
dominus, domini, m., *lord*
domus, us, f. (4), *home, house*
donec, conj., *until, while, as long as*
donum, -i, n. (2), *gift*
dulcedo, -dinis, f. (3), *sweetness*
dulcis, -e, (3), adj., *sweet*
dum, adv., *while*
duplex, adv., *twofold*
duplicare (1), *to divide*

E

ecce, *behold, look*
ecclesia, -ae, f. (1), *church, assembly*
edo, edere, edi, esus (1), *to eat*
effectus, -us, m. (4), *effect, result*
efficere, (3), *to effect, make*
ego, pers. pron., *I*
egredior, dep. (3), *to go out*
eja, interj., *well then*
eligere (3), *to choose*
emittere (3), *to send forth*
enarrare (1), *to tell, divulge*
enim, conj., *for*
episcopus, -i, m. (2), *bishop*
equus, -i, m. (2), *horse*
ergo, adv., *therefore*
erigere (3), *to raise, to lift up*
error, erroris, m. (3), *error*
esse, irr. vb., *to be*
essentia, -ae, f. (1), *essence, nature*
esurire (4), *to be hungry*

et, conj., *and*
etsi, conj., *although*
evadere (3), *to evade*
evangelicus, -a, -um, adj., *evangelical*
evangelium, -i, n. (2), *gospel, good news*
ex, prep., *out of, from*
excedere (3), *to exced*
exercitus, -us, m. (4), *army*
explere (2), *to fill up, complete*
exponere (3), *to explain, expose*
exsaltare (1), *to lift up, exalt*
exsul, exsulis, m. f. (3), *exile*
exsultare (1), *to lift up, exult*

F

facere (4), *to make or do*
facies, -ei, f. (5), *face*
famulus, -i, m. (2), *servant, slave*
fatuitas, -tatis, f. (3), *foolishness*
fatuus, -a, -um, adj., *foolish*
felicitas, -tatis, f. (3), *happiness*
ferreus, -a, -um, adj., *ironlike*
festivitas, -tatis, f. (3), *festivity*
festus, -i, m. (2), *feast*
fictilis, -e, adj., *earthen*
ficus, -us, f. (4), *fig tree*
fidelitas, -tatis, f. (3), *faithfulness, fidelity*
fieri, irr. vb., *to become*
filia, -ae, f. (1), *daughter*
filius, -i (2), *son*
filum, -i, n. (2), *thread*
fio, fieri, factus sum, passive of *facere*
firmare (1), *to fix*
flagellatio, -onis, f. (3), *whipping, scourging*
flere (2), *to weep*
foramen, -is, n. (3), *opening, eye*
forte, conj., *perhaps*
fovea, -ae, f. (1), *pit*
frenus, -i, m. (2), *bridle*

fructus, fructus, m., *fruit*
frustrare (1), *to cheat*
funus, -eris, n. (3), *burial*
fur, furis, m. (3), *thief, robber*

G

gaudiosus, -, -um, adj., *joyful*
gemere (3), *to sigh, to groan*
generatio, generationis (3),
    generation
genetrix, genitiricis, f.,
    generator, parent
genus, generis, n. (3), *kind,
    genus, family, clan, race*
gignere, genui, genitus (3), *to
    give birth*
gladius, -i, m. (2), *sword*
glorior, gloriari, dep. (1), *to
    glory in, boast*
gloriosus, -a, -um, adj., *glorious*
gratia, gratiae, f., *grace*
gravari, dep. (1), *to weigh on*
gustare (1), *to taste*

H

habere (2), *to have*
habitaculum, -i, n. (2), *dwelling*
habitare (1), *to dwell, live in*
habitatio, -onis f. (3), *home,
    habitation*
habitor, -oris, m. (3), *inhabitant*
haereditas, -tatis, f. (3),
    inheritance
hic, haec, hoc, dem. pron., *this*
hirundo, -inis, f. (3), *a swallow*
hodie, adv., *today*
homilia, -ae, f. (1), *homily*
homo, -minis, m. (3), *man,
    human being*
hora, horae, f. (1), *hour*
horrere (2), *to bristle, to shudder*
hortus, -i, m. (2), *garden*

huiusmodi, *of this kind*
humilis, -e, *humble, lowly*
humilitas, -tatis, f. (3), *humility*
humiliter, adv., *humbly*
hunc, adv., *from here*

I

ibi, adv., *there*
ideo, conj., *therefore*
igitur, adv., *therefore*
ignis, -is, m. (3), *fire*
ille, illa, illud, dem. pron., *that*
illuminare (1), *to illuminate, to
    light*
imago, -inis, f., *image*
immensus, -a, -um, adj., *immense*
immerito, adv., *unworthily*
immo, adv., *indeed, rather*
immortalis, -e, adj., *immortal*
immutare (1), *to change*
impedimentum, -i, n. (2), *obstacle*
impietas, -tatis, f. (3), *impiety*
implere, (2), *to fill up*
imputare (1), *to impute, blame*
in, prep., *in, into*
inanis, -e, adj., *empty, inane*
incarnatio, -onis, f. (3),
    incarnation, enfleshment
incessabilis, -e, adj., *unceasing*
inclytus, -a, -um, adj., *celebrated*
incolere (3), *to inhabit, dwell in*
increpare (1), *to murmur*
inde, *thence*
indigere (2), *to need*
indubitanter, adv., *undoubtedly*
inducare, (1), *to lead into*
inexspectare (1), *not to look for*
inferi, inferorum m. (2), *lower
    places, hell*
infernus, -i, m. (2), *underworld,
    hell*
infirmitas, -tatis, f. (3), *sickness*
ingredior, dep. (3), *to go in*
inimicus, -i, m. (2), *enemy*

iniquitas, iniquitatis, f. (3), *iniquity*

iniustus, -a, -um, adj., *unjust*

injuria, -ae, f. (1), *injury*

inquit, def. vb., *he says*

inscriptio, -onis, f. (3), *inscription*

insidiae, -arum, f. (1), *ambush, wiles*

instare (1), *tو stand around, be present*

intellectus, us, m. (4), *understanding*

intelligibilis, -e, adj., *intelligible*

intendere (3), *to attend, listen*

intercedere (3), *to intercede*

interitus, -us, m. (4), *destruction*

interrogare (1), *to ask*

intrare (1), *to go in*

introire (4), *to go in, enter*

intueor, dep. (2), *to look at, gaze*

inventio, -onis, f. (3), *discovery*

inveterare (1), *to grow old*

invicem, *one another*

ipse, ipsa, ipsum, dem. pron., *that one, very*

ira, -ae, f. (1), *wrath, anger*

is, ea, id, dem. pron., *he, she, it*

iterum, adv., *again*

iurare (1), *to swear*

iusiurandum, -i, n. (2), *oath*

J

jam, adv., *now*

judicare (1), *to judge*

jurare (1), *to swear*

juventus, -tutis, f. (3), *youth*

L

labefactare (1), *to shake, loosen*

lacrima, -ae, f. (1), *tear*

laetitia, -ae, f. (1), *joy*

laetor, laetui, laetus, dep. (1), *to rejoice*

lancea, -ae, f. (1), *spear*

lapis, lapidis, m. (3), *stone*

late, adv., *widely*

latro, -onis, m. (3), *robber, thief*

laudabilis, -e, adj., *praiseworthy*

laudare (1), *to praise*

lectio, -onis, f. (3), *reading*

liberare, (1), *to free, deliver*

licet, conj., *although*

licet, licuit, licitum est, *it is allowed*

logica, -ae, f. (1), *logic*

longanimitas, -tatis, f. (3), *patience*

longe, adv., *far off, at a distance*

loquor, loqui, locutus sum, dep., (3), *to speak*

lucere (2), *to light*

luciferum, -i, n. (2), *morning star*

lucror, dep. (1), *to gain*

lucrum, -i, n. (2), *to gain, profit*

lumen, -inis, n. (3), *light*

lux, lucis, f. (3), *light*

M

mactare (1), *to sacrifice*

macula, -ae, f. (1), *stain*

magis, adv., *rather, more*

magister, -ri, m. (2), *teacher, master*

magistratus, -us, m. (4), *magistracy, office*

magnificare (1), *to praise highly*

magnus, magna, magnum, *great, large*

majestas, -tatis, f. (3), *grandeur, dignity*

malle, irr., *to prefer*

malum, mali, n. m., *evil*

mandare (1), *to command*

manere (2), *to remain*

manifestus, -a, -um, *evident, manifest*

mansuetudo, -dinis, f. (3), *mildness*

manus, -us, f. (4), *hand*

Maria, Mariae, f., *Mary*

mater, matris, f., *mother*

maxilla, -ae, f. (1), *cheek*

maxime, adv., *especially, chiefly*

maximus, -, -um, adj., *greatest, largest*

memorare (1), *to note, to remember*

memoria, -ae, f. (1), *memory*

mens, mentis, f. (3), *mind*

merces, mercedis, f. (3), *reward, pay*

merere (2), *to be worthy*

meritum, -i, n. (2), *reward, desert*

meus, mea, meum, *my, mine*

miles, militis, m. (3), *soldier*

minuo, minere, minui, minutus, (3) *to make smaller, diminish*

miror, dep. (1), *to wonder*

misericordia, -ae, f. *mercy*

misericorditer, adv., *mercifully*

misericors, -cordis, adj., *pitiful, compassionate*

mittere (3), *to send*

modicum, -i, n. (2), *little bit*

modo, adv., *now*

modus, -i, m. (2), *manner, mode*

monere (2), *to warn*

morbus, -i, m. (2), *illness*

morior, mori, mortuus sum, dep., (3), *to die*

mors, mortis, f., *death*

mortuus, -a, -um, *dead*

mulier, muleris, f. (3), *woman*

multiplex, multiplicis, adj., *manifold, multiple*

mulus, -i, m. (2), *mule*

mundare (1), *to clean*

mundus, -i, m. (2), *world*

munus, -eris, n. (3), *gift*

mysterium, -i, n. (2), *mystery*

N

nascor, nasci, natus sum, dep. (3), *to be born*

natio, -onis, f. (3), *nation*

necessarium, -i, n. (2), *necessity*

negotium, -i, n. (2), *business*

nemo, neminis, *no one*

nequeo, nequere, nequivi, nequitus (4), *to be unable*

nimirum, adv., *doubtless, truly*

nisi, *unless*

nobis, ablative of nos, *we, us*

noctua, -ae, f. (1), *nightbird, owl*

nolle, irr., *to wish not*

nomen, -inis, n. (3), *name*

nondum, adv., *not yet*

nos, nobis, pers. pron., *we, us*

noscere (3), *to know*

noster, nostra, adj., *our*

notus, -a, -um, adj., *known*

noxius, -a, -um, adj., *harmful*

numerus, -i, m. (2), *number*

numquid, adv., *never*

nunc, adv., *now*

nuntiare (1), *to announce*

O

obsecrare (1), *to implore, beseech*

obsecratio, -onis, f. (3), *prayer*

obstupescere (3), *to be astounded, become stupid*

obtegere (3), *to cover over*

occidere (4), *to kill*

occurrere (3), *to occur*

oculus, -i, m. (2), *eye*

odire (4), *to hate*

odium, -i, n. (2), *hate*

offere (3), *to offer*

omnipotens, -tentis, adj.,
  almighty
omnis, omne, adj., *all, every*
operatio, -onis, f. (3), *activity,*
  operation
operor, dep. (1), *to work*
opitulor, dep. (1), *to help, assist*
oportet, *it is necessary, fitting*
opportunus, -a, -um, *opportune,*
  fitting
orare, (1), *to pray*
orbis, -is, m. (3), *circle, ring,*
  anything round
ordo, -dinis, m. (3), *order*
orior, oriri, ortus sum, dep. (4),
  to rise
ortus, -us, m. (4), *birth, rising*
ostium, -i, n. (2), *door, entrance*
ovis, ovis, f. (3), *sheep*

P

panis, -is, m. (3), *bread*
pascuum, -i, n. (2), *pasture*
passio, -onis, f. (3), *passion,*
  suffering
pastor, -oris, m. (3), *shepherd*
Pater, patris, m. (3), *father*
patere (2), *to lie open*
patet, *it is evident*
patior, pati, passus sum, dep.
  (3), *to suffer*
patrocinium, -i, n. (2), *patronage*
pauper, pauperis, adj., *poor*
pax, pacis, f. (3), *peace*
peccatum, -i, n., *sin*
peccatum (2), *to sin*
pectus, -oris, n. (3), *breast*
pecunia, -ae, f. (1), *money*
penes, prep., *with*
penetrare (1), *to penetrate*
perambulare (1), *to walk through*
  or around
perdere (3), *to lose*
perducare (1) *to lead to*

perfecte, adv., *perfectly*
perfectus, -a, -um, *perfect,*
  complete
perhibere (2), *to give*
periculum, -i, n. (2), *peril*
perniciosus, -a, -um, adj.,
  harmful, pernicious
pertransire (4), *to pass through,*
  pierce
perversitas, -tatis, f. (3),
  perversity
pes, pedis, m. (3), *foot*
petere (3), *to seek*
philosophus, -i, n. (2),
  philosopher
pipilare (1), *to twitter or cheep*
piscina, -ae, f. (1), *pool*
piscis, -is, m. (3), *fish*
pius, -a, -um, adj., *dutiful, pious*
plane, adv., *plainly, openly*
plangere (3), *to weep, wail*
plebs, plebis, f. (3), *people*
plenitudo, -inis, f. (3), *fullness*
plenus, plena, plenum, adj., *full*
plicare (1), *to fold*
pluo, plere, plevi, pletus (3), *to*
  rain
plusquam, adv., *more than*
poenalis, -e, adj., *punitive, penal*
poenitere (2), *to regret*
ponere (3), *to put, place*
porrigere (3), *to reach out, extend*
porta, -ae., f. (1), *gate*
possibilis, -e, adj., *possible*
posteaquam, adv., *later, after*
potens, potentis, adj., *powerful*
potentia, -ae, f. (1), *power,*
  capacity
potest (from **possum, posse,**
  potui), *it can be*
potestas, -atis, f. (3), *power*
praebere (2), *to offer, to hold out*
praecipere (4), *to order, command*
praepedire (3), *to shackle, fetter*
praeponere (3), *to put before*
praescire (3), *to foretell*

prandium, -i, n. (2), *lunch, meal*
premere (3), *to press*
presentatio, -onis, f. (3), *presenting*
pretiosus, -a, -um, adj., *precious*
princeps, -is, m. (3), *leader, chief*
principaliter, adv., *chiefly*
principatus, -us, m. (4), *primacy*
principium, -i, n. (2), *beginning, principle*
pro, prep., *for, on behalf of*
procedere (3), *to proceed*
proclamare (1), *to proclaim*
prodere (3), *to go forth, advance, promote*
profecto, adv., *indeed, truly*
profundum, -i, n. (2), *depth*
progenies, -ei, f. (5), *descent, race, progeny*
projicere (3), *to throw, cast before or down*
promissio, -onis, f. (3), *promise*
propheta, -ae, (1), *prophet*
proprius, -a, -um, adj., *own, proper*
propter, prep., *on account of*
propterea, adv., *on that account*
protendere (3), *to stretch forth*
publicanus, -i, m. (2), *publican*
puer, -i, m. (2), *boy, child*
pugnum, -i, n. (2), *fight*
pulsare (1), *to knock*
pusillitas, -tatis, f. (3), *smallness*
pusillus, -a, -um, adj., *little*

Q

quaerere (3), *to seek*
qualis, -e, *what kind*
quamdiu, adv., *as long as*
quamvis, adv., *although*
quando, adv., *when*
quandocumque, adv., *whenever*
quantum, *how much?*
quantus, -a, -um, adj., *how much*

quasi, adv., *as if*
quemadmodum, adv., *just as*
qui, quae, quod, rel. pron., *who, which, that*
quia, conj., *because*
quinque, *five*
quippe, conj., *indeed*
quis, quid, interr. pron., *who?*
quisnam, *what then*
quisquis, quaequae, quidquid, pron., *whoever, whichever*
quoad, prep., *as to, with respect to*
quomodo, adv., *how*
quoniam, conj., *since*
quotidianus, -a, -um, *daily*
quotidie, adv., *daily*
quotquot, *however many*

R

radius, -i, m. (2), *ray*
recordare, (1), *to remember*
recordatio, -onis, f. (3), *remembering*
rectus, -a, -um, adj., *right, correct*
reddere (3), *to render, to give*
redimere (3), *to buy back*
refugium, -i, n. (2), *refuge*
regere (3), *to rule*
regina, -ae, f. (1), *queen*
regnum, -i, n. (2), *kingdom*
relaxare (1), *to let go, cede*
relinquere (3), *to let go, relinquish*
reliquus, -a, -um, *remaining, left behind*
remissio, -onis, f. (3), *forgiveness*
remittere (3), *to forgive, remit*
requiescere (3), *to rest, repose*
res, rei, f. (5), *thing, matter*
residuum, -a, -um, adj., *remainder, what is left*
respectus, -us, m. (4), *respect*
respicere (4), *to look to, respect*
respondere (3), *to answer*
resurgere (3), *to rise again*

resurrectio, -onis, f. (3), *resurrection*

retributio, -onis, f. (3), *retribution*

reverentia, -ae, f. (1), *reverence*

rex, regis, m. (3), *king*

roborare (1), *to strengthen*

ros, roris, m. (3), *dew*

rugere (3), *to groan*

rursus, adv., *again*

S

sacerdos, -dotis, m. (3), *priest*

sacramentum, -i, n. (2), *sacred sign, sacrament*

saeculum, -i, n. (2), *to age*

saepe, adv., *often*

salubriter, adv., *healthily*

salus, -utis, f. (3), *safety, salvation*

salutaris, salutare, *salutary,* as noun, *salvation*

salvator, -oris, m. (3), *savior*

salvus, -a, -um, *safe, saved*

sanctificare, (1), *to hallow, bless, make holy*

sanctitas, -tatis, f. (3), *sanctity, holiness*

sanctus, sancta, sanctum, adj., *holy*

sanguis, -inis, m. (3), *blood*

sapiens, -entis, m. (3), *sage, wise one*

sapientia, -ae, f. (1), *wisdom*

saxeus, -a, -um, adj., *stony*

scabellum, -i, n. (2), *footstool*

sceptrum, -i, n. (2), *scepter*

scilicet, adv., *namely*

scindere (3), *to sunder*

scire (4), *to know*

scribere (2), *to write*

secundo, adv., *secondly*

secundum, *according to*

securus, -a, -um, adj., *safe, secure*

sed, conj., *but*

sedere (2), *to seat, sit*

sedes, sedis, f. (3), *seat*

semen, seminis, n. (3), *seed*

semper, adv., *always*

sempiternus, -a, -um, adj., *sempiternal*

senex, adj., *old*

sepelire, (4), *to bury*

sepultus, -a, -um, *buried*

sermo, -onis, m. (3), *discourse, talk*

serpens, -entis, f. (3), *snake*

servare (1), *to serve*

sicut, adv., *just as*

signare (1), *to mark, designate*

signum, -i, n. (2), *sign*

similis, -e, adj., *similar*

simpliciter, adv., *absolutely, simply*

sine, prep., *without*

singulus, -a, -um, adj., *each, every*

sinus, -us, m. (4), *bosom*

solemnitas, -tatis, f. (3), *celebration*

sollicitus, -a, -um, *strongly moved, stirred up*

solus, -a, -um, adj., *alone*

solvere (3), *to loosen, break up*

sordes, -is, f. (3), *dirt, filty*

sperare (1), *to hope*

spes, -ei, f. (5), *hope*

spina, -ae, f. (1), *thorn*

spiritus, spiritus, n. (4), *spirit*

splendidus, -a, -um, adj., *shining*

splendor, -oris, m. (3), *splendor*

stare (1), *to stand*

stella, -ae, f. (1), *star*

stultus, -a, -um, adj., *stupid*

stupere (2), *to stun*

sub, prep., with. abl., *under*

subdere (3), *to set under*

subere (3), *to go under, to climb*

subindicare (1), *to intimate, indicate*

subministrare (1), *to furnish, supply*

subsequor, subsequi, subsecutus sum, dep. (3), *to follow after*

subtiliter, adv., *minutely, subtly*

subvenire (3), *to assist*

superare (1), *to overcome, surpass*

superbus, -a, -um, *proud*

superfluus, -a, -um, adj., *overflowing, superfluous*

supplere (2), *to fill up, make complete, supply*

supportare (1), *to support*

suscipere (3), *to take up, to take on*

suspirare (1), *to breathe deeply, to sigh*

T

tacere (2), *to be silent*

tamen, conj., *yet now*

tantum, adv., *only*

tantus, -a, -um, adj., *of such size, so great*

tela, -ae, f. (1), *a web, what is woven*

templum, -i, n. (2), *temple*

tempus, -oris, n. (3), *time*

tentatio, tentationis, f. (3), *temptation, trial*

tentorium, -i, n. (2), *tent*

terra, -ae, f. (1), *earth*

terrenus, -a, -um, adj., *earthly*

tertius, -a, -um, *third*

testare (1), *to give witness*

testis, -is, m. (3), *witness*

texo, texere, texui, textus, (3), *to weave*

textor, -oris, m. (3), *weaver*

thesaurum, -i, n., *treasury*

thus, thuris, n. (3), *incense*

timere (2), *to fear*

timor, -oris, m. (3), *fear*

tollere, sustuli, sublatus, irr. (3), *to raise up*

torrens, -entis, m. (3), *torrent*

totus, -a, -um, *whole, all*

tradere (3), *to treat, pass on*

transire (3), *to pass by or through*

tribuere (3), *to allot, share, bestow*

tribulatio, -onis, f. (3), *trouble*

tributum, -i, n. (2), *tribute*

triumphus, -i, (2), *to triumph*

tu, pers. pron., *you, thou*

tueor, tueri, tuitus sum, dep. (2), *to look at, behold*

tumultus, -us, m. (4), *tumult*

tunc, adv., *then*

turba, -ae, f. (1), *crowd*

turbare (1), *to disturb*

tuus, tua, tuum, adj., *your (singular of **vester, vestra, vestrum**)*

U

ulterius, adv., *any longer, further*

ultimus, -a, -um, adj., *ultimate*

unde, *whence*

unicus, -a, -um, adj., *unique, only*

unigenitus, -a, -um, adj., *only begotten*

universus, -a, -um, *all*

unusquisque, pron., *whoever, anyone*

ut, adv., *as*

ut, conj., *that, so that* (with subjunctive)

uterus, -i, m. (2), *womb*

utique, *at any rate, certainly, indeed*

utor, uti, usus sum, dep. (3), *to use*

V

vadere (3), *to go*

valles, -is, f. (3), *valley*

vas, vasis, n. (3), *vessel*
vehementer, adv., *vehemently*
velle, irr., *to wish*
venerare (1), *to venerate*
venia, -ae, f. (1), *grace, favor*
venire (4), *to come*
venter, ventris, n. m., *womb*
veraciter, adv., *truly*
verax, veracis, adj., *true, truthful*
verbum, -i, n. (2), *word*
veritas, -tatis, f. (3), *truth*
vero, adv., *indeed, truly*
versutia, -ae, f. (1), *cunning, craftiness*
verus, -a, -um, adj., *true*
vetustus, -a, -um, adj., *old*
via, -ae, f. (1), *way*
vicinus, -a, -um, adj., *neighboring*
vigilare (1), *to keep vigil*

vigor, -is, m. (3), *strength*
vinculum, -i, n. (2), *bond, chain*
virginitas, -tatis, f. (3), *virginity*
virgo, virginis, f. (3), *virgin*
virtus, -tutis, f. (3), *power, virtue*
vis, vim, vi, pl. **vires,** f. *force, power, strength*
viscus, -eris, n. (3), *usually plural, viscera, entrails*
visitatio, -onis, f. (3), *visit*
vitium, -i, n. (2), *vice*
vivus, -a, -um, *living, alive*
vocare (1), *to call*
vocatio, -onis, f. (3), *calling*
vociferor, dep. (1), *to cry loudly, shout*
voluntas, -tatis, f. (3), *will*
vos, pers. pron., *you*